Messiah REVEALED
in SHAVUOT

by

Hannah Nesher

VOICE for
Israel

ISBN# 978-0-9733892-1-0

For speaking engagements please contact Hannah:

Hannah Nesher, Voice for Israel
Suite #313- 11215 Jasper Ave.
Edmonton, Alberta
T5K 0L5 Canada

www.voiceforisrael.net

Cover design by James Vanderwekken - jvnderwe@hotmail.com
Cover photo by Chris Potter

DEDICATION

To the God of my fathers, Avraham, Yitzchak and Yaacov,

יהוה
אהיה אשר אהיה

To You whose name says

You will be whoever You will be –

Thanks for being all I have ever needed!

And to Your Son and Messiah Y'shuah

ישׁוע

For your obedience to the Father

For being led like a lamb to the slaughter

For pouring out your soul unto death

So that I could live!

A Special Thank You

I would like to say *todah rabah* (thanks very much) and publicly acknowledge my debt of gratitude towards some of the many people who helped with this work.

First of all, to my mother and father who gave me life. Thank you for your courage in training up this daughter of yours through all our ups and downs. Although we may not always agree on theology, your love has remained constant.

To David, for applying your excellent technical skills to help bring this book to publication. Thank you for your love, encouragment and steadfast faith - and for the gift of our two wonderful children.

To my children, Clayton, Courtney, Timothy, Liat, and Avi-ad, who each supplied material and inspiration for my writing. Thanks for your patience with the crazy times in our family - for loving and forgiving me. Big hugs to Clayton for his great technical support.

To our ministry partners for your faithful love, fervent prayers and generous support. May you be fully rewarded by the God of Israel under whose wings you have taken refuge - Ruth 2:12

To James Vanderwekken for his awesome graphic design work and technical support. You are a treasure!

To Denis Vanderwekken & his late wife, Corrie for their friendship, support, and help in the journey. Corrie - I miss you!
To Marilyn for your intercession & willingness to proofread.

Most of all, to the Holy Spirit (Ruach Hakodesh), for giving me the inspiration, motivation, and words to write.

Todah rabah! (thanks so much!) תודה רבה

CONTENTS

Introduction...9

1   **The Hellenization of the Body of Messiah**........13
     Come Out of Her, My People..............................14
     Whoever Breaks the
     Least of These Commandments.........................15
     Is it Paul's Fault?...16
     Jesus and Paul Were Not Christians..................18
     The Ghost of Marcion.......................................18
     The Council of Nicea...21
     Jesus Kicked Off Christian Campus?................22
     A Deadly Mixture..22
     The Worst Divorce in History............................23

1   **One Root**...**25**
     Faith and Works..26
     I Bring Not Peace But A Sword.........................27
     Harmony of Law and Grace..............................29
     Worshipping in Spirit and in Truth....................30
     Torah is not Enough..30
     Called but Impotent?...31
     Entering into the Holy of Holies.......................33

The Spirit Brings Life............................35

Loving One Another.............................36

Filled with the Holy Spirit.....................38

3   **The Prophetic Significance
     of the Book of Ruth**........................**40**

Replacement Theology..........................46

Times of the Gentiles Fulfilled................48

Role of Gentile Believers
- No Longer Foreigners.........................52

Understanding the Jewishness of the Gospel............55

The Gift of the Holy Spirit.....................57

4   **Anti-Torah Attitudes -
     Does Grace Nullify the Law?**.........**59**

Is the Torah Abolished?.........................61

The Sh'ma - the Law on Our Hearts............65

Sealed With Blood...............................68

Sacrificial Law Fulfilled........................69

Blessing or Cursing.............................71

Peter's Vision - People or Food?...............73

The Jerusalem Council...........................76

5   **One Torah**.....................................**78**

Bowing in the House of Rimmon..............81

Only One Law....................................82

The Sign of the Spirit: Obedience..............84

Paul's Letters....................................85

Zealous for the Law.............................86

Mount Sinai - A Betrothal......................87

Sh'ma Yisrael...89
Salvation By Grace..91

6   **Re-Discovering Torah.................................94**
The Final Triumph of the Torah........................100
Israel Returning to the Kingdom......................100
The Olive Tree..101
Strychnine Disguised as Candy........................102
Jesus and Mary Statues Take Priority..............103

Appendix...107
Bibliography...109

Introduction

Two highly significant events occurred on Pentecost
(Shavuot): the giving of the law (Torah) and the giving of
the Spirit. Most Jewish people traditionally consider this
Feast of the Lord as the time when Moses received the Ten
Commandments, the tablets of the covenant, on Mt. Sinai.
It is also traditionally considered by most Christians as the
'birth of the Church', the time that God poured out His Holy
Spirit upon the apostles. The concepts of law and grace have
been long-debated and a resurgence of the controversy is
occurring with a renewal of an interest in Torah[1] on the part
of many people of God searching for their Jewish-Hebraic
roots. I hope and pray that this book will help to clarify
these issues rather than further muddy the waters. This one
thing I pray, that the Holy Spirit would you keep lies and
falsehood far from us. (Prov.30:8) I offer you a Messianic
Jewish perspective of these two treasured gifts of the Lord -
His Torah and Spirit through this commentary on Pentecost
(the Feast of Shavuot).

---

1   The Torah was according to tradition, given to Israel on Shavuot.

Scriptural Background

God proclaims Shavuot as one of His appointed times (moadim) to celebrate.

> "From the day after the Sabbath, the day you brought the sheaf of the wave offering, count off seven full weeks (Shavuot). Count off fifty days up to the day after the seventh Sabbath, and then present an offering of new grain to the Lord…On that same day you are to proclaim a sacred assembly and do no regular work. This is to be a lasting ordinance for the generations to come, wherever you live. When you reap the harvest of your land, do not reap to the very edges of your field or gather the gleanings of your harvest. Leave them for the poor and the alien. I am the Lord your God." (Lev. 23:15-22)

> "You shall count seven weeks from the time you begin to put the sickle to the standing grain. Then celebrate Shavuot to the Lord your God by giving a freewill offering in proportion to the blessings the Lord your god has given you. And rejoice before the Lord your God at the place he will choose as a dwelling for his Name – you, your sons and daughter, your menservants and maidservants, the Levites in your towns, and the aliens, the fatherless and the widows living among you. Remember that you were slaves in Egypt, and follow carefully these decrees." (Deut. 16:9-12)

What is Torah?

The word *Torah* comes from the roots yara, which means to shoot, aim, or point to, and mora, meaning teacher. Therefore, the Torah is God's instructions to His people. The teachings within teach us how to live on this earth and point us to eternal life through Yeshua. The Torah, in its strictest sense, includes the five books of Moses: Genesis (B'reisheet), Exodus (Shmot), Leviticus (Vaykira), Numbers (Bamidbar), and Deuteronomy (D'varim). However, Yeshua and Paul both quoted from other books of the Bible and called them Torah (law).

"Yeshua answered them, "Is it not written in your Law (Torah), 'I said, 'You are gods"? (John 10:34)

The quote referred to is found in Psalm 82:6.

In the Law (Torah) it is written:

"With men of other tongue and other lips I will speak to this people…'" (1 Cor. 14:21)

This quote Paul refers to as law is from Isaiah 28:11.

The Tanakh is a Hebrew name for all the books of the Old Testament. It is an acronym: **T-N-KH** which is an abbreviation for: **T**orah, **N**eviim (Prophets) and **K**tuvim (Writings - Psalms, Proverbs, etc).

Observant Orthodox Jews consider another whole compilation of writings as 'Torah'. These are called the 'oral law' and include the Talmud, Mishnah, and Gemorrah, comprised of rabbinical interpretations of scriptures. Many consider the oral law of equal weight and authority as the written Torah and spend the majority of their time and study in these books, sometimes to the exclusion of the written word itself. Most followers of Yeshua do not accept the Talmud as 'law' and rely upon the written scriptures that comprise both the Tanakh and the Brit Hadashah (New Testament).

CHAPTER ONE

THE HELLENIZATION OF THE BODY OF MESSIAH

The English translation of the word Shavuot is 'weeks', therefore the English name – Feast of Weeks. Most Christians are more familiar with the Greek-based word meaning fifty (50)– Pentecost.[2] The fact that many people of the Lord do not know either the Hebrew or the English translation of the feast is evidence of the widespread hellenization of the Christian Church. It was this same hellenization of Judaism, the infiltration of Greek/Roman/pagan influence that the Maccabees desperately fought against, a victory celebrated today as the festival of Chanukah.

King Antiochus at first encouraged assimilation into Greek culture and later forbade all expressions of Jewish identity. He commanded the worship of pagan Greek gods and defiled the holy temple by sacrificing pigs on the altar, thereby foreshadowing to us the actions of the coming anti-Christ. The Maccabees rebelled against this defilement of their faith in the one true God – the God of Israel, of Abraham, Isaac, and Jacob. God gave these few brave Jewish men victory over the entire Greek/Babylonian forces. Over the centuries since the time of the Messiah, the people of God

---

2 Count fifty days to the day after the seventh Sabbath. (Lev. 23:16)

have once again fallen under this pagan, anti-God influence through compromise, deception, and ignorance.

Christmas and Easter, widely celebrated as 'Christian holidays', contain roots in Babylon. They were both days special to worship pagan gods and goddesses. These celebrations were characterized by drunkenness and sexual immorality. The Sunday day of meeting originates from the pagan 'Esteemed Day of the Sun', a day to worship the sun god.

"If the root is holy, so are the branches."
(Rom.11:16)

If we turn this scripture around, if the root is unholy and pagan, how can the branches be holy?

Come Out of Her, My People

How did the body of the Messiah, (who have as their head Yeshua[3] an observant Jew), absorb pagan elements into their religion, when God has specifically forbidden His people to worship in the way of the pagan peoples around them; to be a separate and holy people unto Him? If the Church is the Bride of Christ, how can the bridegroom marry His beloved while she still lives in Babylon? In the account of Isaac's arranged marriage to Rebecca, she was willing to follow Abraham's servant out of Mesopotamia (Babylon), in order to marry her bridegroom. Are we also willing to follow Yeshua, even if it means leaving all that we have known and all that has become familiar to us in 'Babylon'? Will you make the decision to follow His leading out of false religion and spiritual adultery back to the Land of Promise even if none go with you? *"I have decided, to follow Jesus...though none go with me, still I will follow."*

---
3 Yeshua is Jesus' Hebrew name.

The Christian Church has, for the most part, adopted an anti-Torah (anti-nomian) attitude, a belief that because of Jesus and the new covenant, we are therefore released from the law of the old covenant. What does this mean? Does this mean that we are no longer required to keep the laws and commandments of God? Are we now free to commit adultery and murder? Some would then claim that we are obligated to keep the Ten Commandments but not the other laws such as the feasts or dietary laws. If the Ten Commandments are still in effect, then what about the fourth commandment regarding the Sabbath? How is it that the people of God have given themselves the liberty to pick and choose at will which laws they are released from and which are still binding? Is the Bible a kind of 'salad bar' in which we can choose what we find tasty and disregard what doesn't look good in our eyes? I would like to examine and challenge this negative attitude with regards to Torah, which is usually erroneously called 'law'. In fact, Torah does not mean 'law' with all its negative connotations and an innate desire to be free of its restrictions. Instead, Torah means teaching; it is God's guidance for our lives.

Whoever Breaks the Least of These Commandments...

Early Believers all lived and worshipped in the Biblical way celebrating the Feasts of the Lord, honouring Shabbat (the Sabbath) and keeping it holy. Yeshua specifically told us that He did not come to abolish the Torah and that no one should teach people not to keep God's commandments (Matt. 5:1719). In fact, the Lord clearly specifies that those who break even the least of the commandments of God and teach others to do the same will be the least in the Kingdom. Not everyone will be equal in the Kingdom of God. As for me, I want to be as close to the Lord as possible, therefore

I will, at the risk of being called a Judaizer, teach others to keep the commandments of God, not the falsehood that they are 'free from the law'. If I am a Judaizer for teaching people to keep the Torah, then so was Yeshua, for this is also what He taught, and what He commissioned us to do after He left this earth to sit at the right hand of the Father.

> **"Go therefore and make disciples of all the nations,... teaching them to observe all things that I have commanded you."**
> (Matt. 28:19, 20)

The Jews have always known that the Messiah would teach the correct interpretation of the Torah, but then when He showed up, the religious leaders didn't appreciate His challenge to their man-made rules and regulations, taught as if they were doctrines of God.

Is It Paul's Fault?

Many people, even traditional Jewish sources, will admit that Yeshua never intended to create a religion that taught 'freedom from the law', but instead they cast the blame for this apostasy on the apostle Paul.[4]

But is this fair? Is it true that Paul did not keep the law and taught others also not to keep it? Even in Biblical times, Paul had to squash nasty rumours people were spreading about him that he was telling the Jewish believers to disobey the commands of Moses and not circumcise their children. He said there was no truth to these rumours and that he himself, along with tens of thousands of Jewish believers

---

4 Prager Dennis and Telushkin Joseph, *'The Nine Questions People Ask About Judaism'*

were all zealous for the law.

"Then everybody will know there is no truth in these reports about you, but that you yourself are living in obedience to the law (Torah)." (Acts 21:20-24)

Some Bibles entitle Acts chapter 9, 'The Conversion of Paul'. The inference here is that Rabbi Shaul, a loyal, Torah-observant Jew, experienced a miraculous encounter with Jesus, and therefore 'converted' to Christianity. In fact, through a sovereign move of God, who literally knocked him off his horse, Shaul (Paul's Hebrew name), finally realized that Yeshua is actually the Messiah.[5]

Previously, Shaul had been raiding synagogues to arrest Messianic Jews worshipping there. (Acts 9:2) Messianic Judaism was considered a stream of Judaism, not a separate religion. The term 'Christian' was a term first mentioned in Acts 11:26, and was applied exclusively to Gentiles coming to faith in the Messiah. Christianity has transformed Rav Shaul into the apostle Paul, the champion of 'freedom from the law'. But Paul would not have tried to accomplish what Yeshua warned against – the abolition of Torah. Some believe that Paul corrected the problem of legalism amongst Messianic Jews. One Christian informed me that *"Paul exemplified a Jew who was set free from Judaism."*
Obviously, this is a false accusation, since Paul went to great pains to prove that he did actually live in accordance with the Torah. (Acts 21:2024). Paul not only participated in a Nazarite vow; he also offered sacrifices in the temple,

---

5 Chaimberlin, Rick Aharon *'The "Conversion" of Saul of Tarsus'*, Petach Tikvah (Door of Hope), Jan-March 2001, vol. 19, No. 1, pg. 21. For a copy of this excellent publication write: 165 Doncaster Road, Rochester, NY, 14623, USA

which is what the vow required for purification. This is shocking – that Paul offered a sacrifice in the temple even after Yeshua's death!

Jesus and Paul Were Not Christians

Obviously, Shaul did not 'convert' to Christianity. (Actually, neither did Yeshua!). Shaul said,

"I have committed no offense either against the Law of the Jews or against the temple or against Caesar." (Acts 25:8)

Would he have lived one way, but encouraged others to live another?

Indeed, many Christians quote the words of Paul to justify their anti-law, anti-Jewish, doctrinal beliefs. Rather than blaming the apostle Paul, who suffered so much to further the good news of salvation through the Messiah Yeshua, I would like to examine the true origin of the anti-Torah attitude that is so prevalent in the Christian Church today.

The Ghost of Marcion

Daniel Botkin, author of the Gates of Eden newsletter, has written several booklets, one of which, is entitled 'The Ghost of Marcion'.[6] It examines the tendency in mainstream Christianity to de-emphasize the Old Testament and put a disproportionate amount of emphasis on Paul's epistles. I

6 For a copy of this excellent publication or newsletter, write: Gates of Eden, PO Box 2257, East Peoria, IL, 61611-0257. Great thanks to Daniel Botkin for his insightful research and information. Tape and video also available from the above address.

attended a meeting of Christian home-schoolers, where it was announced that someone would offer language lessons in German. When I suggested a class in Hebrew, the language of our scriptures, I was refused. Why? "Because the Old Testament is dead." Where does this attitude come from?

Since Paul's writings make up only approximately 5% of the Bible, and certainly do not carry more weight or authority than the Old Testament or the rest of the New Testament, why so much emphasis on the letters of Paul? This is especially puzzling in light of the clear warning from Peter that these letters are hard to understand and we are in danger of misinterpreting them, to our own destruction.

> **"...Paul, according to the wisdom given to him, has written to you... in which are some things hard to understand, which untaught and unstable people twist to their own destruction, as they do also the rest of the Scriptures."** (2 Pet. 3:15, 16)

Some Christians, however, seem more intent on following their interpretation of Paul's writings in these letters than even the words of Yeshua Himself. This led me to write a particularly scathing paragraph in an e-mail about this very subject after someone tried to 'teach me Paul' and 'set me free from my bondage to the Torah' one too many times. Entitled, *"Watch out! The Paulians are coming"* it caused us to lose the support of a congregation which took offence. This is an emotionally volatile issue, since it slices very close to the core of Christian doctrine of today, even taking a stand against the 'Father of lies'.

How did these anti-Torah attitudes come into existence? Historically, the original apostles were all Jews, who had all studied the teachings of the Torah and prophets since they were small children. Even today in Israel, children from religious families begin memorizing Hebrew scripture from as young as three years old. However, due to a variety of circumstances, the leaders of the Messianic community who replaced the apostles were mostly Gentiles from a pagan background with little or no understanding of Old Testament Scriptures.

One person, in particular, planted seeds of hostility towards the Torah. The heretic Marcion, who lived in the second half of the Second Century, taught that *"the entire Old Testament should be rejected because it belonged to an evil, inferior God, and not to the God revealed by Jesus of Nazareth."*[7] Marcion's God never displays hostility or wrath, as does the stern, fierce, 'Old Testament God.' This 'New Testament God' is never offended or angry; He is merely kind. And He certainly does not expect obedience to His laws. Or at least He would not punish if one were disobedient. This sounds foolish to us, but is it so farfetched? I have heard many claim that God would never destroy the Arab population for their hatred and violence against Israel (even though God's Word says He will). Why would God never do this? "Because He is a God of love." We must be very careful that our faith in God is not a deadly concoction of a kind of 'New Age' mixture of truth with lies.

Marcion was also decidedly anti-Jewish and rejected any New Testament writings that spoke favourably of Jewish practices. Paul, according to Marcion, was the only apostle who could be trusted. Marcion's pro-Paul, anti-Jewish churches spread amongst the predominantly non-Jewish population of the Roman Empire, and soon became a major threat to the Messianic faith. It is clear that Marcion's anti-Semitic, pro-Paul heresy never completely died out, but only became absorbed (in a more subtle form) into the mainstream

---

7   Botkin, Daniel, The Ghost of Macrion page 2

Gentile Christian Church. The ghost of Marcion lives on today.

The Council of Nicea

Another major factor in the development of a non-Jewish, anti-Torah, pre-dominantly Gentile religion called Christianity, is the Church of Constantinople, led by the Roman emperor, Constantine. The following is a profession from the Church of Constantinople, which Jews had to affirm if they wanted to join the holy community of the Jewish Messiah, Yeshua:

> *"I renounce all customs, rites, legalism, unleavened breads and sacrifices of lambs of the Hebrews, and all the other feasts of the Hebrews, sacrifices, prayers, aspersions, purifications, sanctifications and propitiations, and fasts, and new moons, and Sabbaths, and superstitions, and hymns and chants and observances and synagogues, and the food and drink of the Hebrews; in one word, I renounce absolutely everything Jewish, every law, rite and custom..."* [8]

Can you fathom the absurdity of this statement? How would Yeshua, a Torah observant Jew, respond to this? He who observed Passover (unleavened breads), Shabbat (Sabbath), kashrut (Biblical dietary laws), and prayed and worshipped in the synagogues – would he also be cast out of the Church? Is Yeshua really head of this body? And yet this attitude still exists in the Church today. Many Gentile

---

8 Stern, David H., *'Restoring the Jewishness of the Gospel'*, Jewish New Testament Publications, pg. 8

Christians, when confronted with the challenge to keep the Torah, say, *"I am not required to keep all these 'Jewish laws '"*, as if the Jews made them up rather than the God they serve!

Jesus Kicked off Christian Campus?

A man once related a true story to me of visiting a Christian Bible college to lead a prayer-for-Israel group. Being a Jewish Believer, he used a tallit and also wore a kippah (men's head covering). One professor confronted him and demanded he leave the campus, since only 'Christians' could minister there. When this man asked the professor if Yeshua (Jesus) a Jew would also be kicked off campus, the man's face absolutely blanched.

"I never thought of that", the Christian Bible college professor replied, *"Thank you."*

A Deadly Mixture

Some Christians remain confused or even offended by Jewish followers in Yeshua who also keep the Torah, although this was norm in the first centuries in the Body of Messiah. It was, in the fourth century, when the Gentiles had outnumbered the Jewish believers and had taken over the 'Church' that the Torah was basically outlawed. This was 'canonized' at a particular meeting of Gentile Christians called the Council of Nicea. It was at this time that the Roman emperor, Constantine, declared Christianity the official religion of the Roman Empire. In order to create unity amongst the many and diverse people groups of the Empire, Constantine incorporated many of their pagan practices and customs into this 'religion'. This change in the Biblical faith of Yeshua and the first century disciples occurred in direct rebellion against the command of God,

> **"Do not worship the Lord your God in 'their' ways."** (Deut. 12:4)

This ungodly, unbiblical call for 'unity' in the Church is reminiscent of the call for unity to build the tower of Babel (Gen. 11:4), or Alexander the Great's call for unity in his empire, *"That they may all be one people"*. To create this unity, God is left out of the picture. The spirit of the anti-Christ rules, which attempts to change the law and times.

> **"He shall speak pompous words against the Most High, shall persecute the saints of the Most High, and shall intend to change times and law."** (Dan. 7:25)

The Worst Divorce in History

Because of centuries of wrong teachings and the 'shepherds leading the people astray', most in the Church just don't quite know what to make of the Torah. One of the greatest tasks that we face today is to restore a right view of the Torah to the Christian Church. This anti-Torah attitude in the Church has had a devastating effect upon evangelization of the Jewish people, to whom we are commissioned to share Yeshua with first.

> **"For I am not ashamed of the gospel of Messiah, for it is the power of God to salvation for everyone who believes, for the Jew first and also for the Greek."** (Rom. 1:16)

The Jews were entrusted with the very oracles of God.

They defended the Torah at times with their lives to ensure its survival. The Torah is the heart of the Jewish nation. It was at Mount Sinai that Israel was betrothed to God through the giving of the Torah. To know that Christians are not devoted to Torah, nor obedient to it, but are rather contemptuous of 'the law', considering themselves 'above' or 'free from' the law, causes an incredible breach. It says to the Jew that Christians have nothing relevant to say to them about one of the most important issues of their faith. This has created the most tragic divorce of all time – that between the Jewish people and those who follow the Jewish Messiah, Yeshua.

CHAPTER TWO

ONE ROOT

God planted for himself a vine, that is Israel, and tended it carefully with love. But that vine did not produce the fruit for which it was intended. Within the Christian Church exist a teaching that for their sins, Israel was cut off from covenant with God, that the Church is now 'spiritual Israel'. This is called replacement theology. In actuality, there is only one tree, not two, and that tree is Israel. There is only a new covenant promised to the house of Israel and the house of Judah (Jer. 31:31). What about the position of Gentiles?

"...were at that time separated from Messiah, alienated from the commonwealth of Israel, and strangers to the covenants of promise, having no hope and without God in the world." (Eph. 2:12)

But through the blood of a Jewish Messiah, the wild branches (Gentiles) were "brought near" (Eph. 2:13), and are now included in the commonwealth of Israel. They are not a replacement for Israel, but rather co-partakers in the covenant that God promised to Israel. God does not desire two separate people, but 'one new man'. This will require a 'repairing of the breach' – an undoing of the damage caused by the arrogance and pride of the wild branches towards the natural branches who were *temporarily* cut off until the time of the fullness of the Gentiles. (Rom. 11:2527) For God's covenants are unbreakable and His gifts and callings irrevocable towards the Jewish people.

Faith and Works

One of the major differences dividing Judaism and Christianity is the issue of law and grace (works and faith). In Judaism, one's actions are generally more important than faith. According to evangelical, charismatic Christianity, the law is done away with and faith becomes the central demand. I have heard it preached from the pulpit that the law is 'crap, garbage, and refuse'. Shortly thereafter, this church split. Another Christian pastor said that once anyone has recited the sinner's prayer, they are saved and going to heaven no matter how they live their lives afterwards on this earth. One of his devoted choir members abandoned her husband and three small children to run off with her partner in adultery.

The Torah is seen as something obsolete and of little use to many Christians. But was this really the form of religion of the earliest followers of Yeshua? After Yeshua's death, the disciples continued to attend and pray at the regularly scheduled hours in the synagogues on Shabbat (Acts 2:46; 3:1). There were no separate services for the Greeks on Sunday mornings and evenings. Peter scrupulously kept the Biblical dietary laws. (Acts 10:14). If Yeshua had taught him to break them, surely he would have done so. Although most people hold the black and white view that circumcision is not a prerequisite for salvation, this was not a clear-cut issue for the early believers. Some taught that circumcision, as a sign of the Abrahamic covenant, was a requirement for those of Abraham's spiritual seed as well. (Acts 15;1; Gal. 2:12) This was an issue of great controversy, since the Torah was well respected, honoured and obeyed by the early believers.

> **"You see, brother, how many myriads of Jews there are who have believed, and they are all zealous for the law."** (Acts 21:20)

I Bring Not Peace But A Sword...

Whether or not we, as followers of God and believers in Yeshua, are to 'keep the Torah' is a potentially divisive issue – even between husbands and wives. Sometimes a couple is blessed and the partner who does not believe in keeping Torah will receive a sudden revelation of the truth in this matter and the two will walk together in unity and agreement. I am reminded of two examples in particular. One sister came to the first week of a series we were teaching on 'Examining the Jewish Roots of Christianity'. The next week, she dragged in her husband. She became enthused, but he was doubtful, cautious. In time, they attended another series of seminars we presented. The husband came to me several times with letters from the quotations of Paul. Finally, I just prayed for him that the Holy Spirit would answer all of his questions and doubts. The next night, he had a vivid dream in which his deceased grandmother told him he was on the right track. His beloved grandmother represented someone who watched over his welfare in truth and love. This was the confirmation he needed. The couple has since gone on to become leaders in the teaching of Torah to home groups in their area.

Another sister was so on fire about this Torah after attending a weekend 'Shabbat' retreat that she asked to borrow all of our materials to photocopy – a task that took her hours! Her husband, however, was reluctant. He argued, *"Our faith is a simple one, why are you trying to make it so complicated with all of this?"* And *"If living without Torah has been good enough for Christianity for two thousand years, why is it not good enough for us now?"* he exclaimed in frustration. None of his wife's answers gave him peace.

One night, however, he watched a video presentation and suddenly jumped up like a lightning bolt hit him, shouting, *"I get it! Now I get it!"* This couple has also gone on to form a thriving, home fellowship group in their area to teach the Biblical roots of the Christian faith.

Others are not so fortunate and it's not always the husband who objects. One brother in the Lord corresponded for a period of time and thanked us profusely for 'opening his eyes' to the truth. He was hungry and eager to learn more. One day, however, I received a one-line question about the Bible. I answered in my usual, long-winded fashion, thinking it strange that his letter was so uncharacteristically brief. It was his wife who had sent the question and answered back with a scathing reply that it's fine and dandy to be interested in these 'Jewish things', but that *"none of the early believers lived according to the law"*. (False) She also warned me to be careful what I wrote to her husband from now on. (The right of Israel to the land.) Sadly, for the sake of marital harmony I suppose, this man submitted to his wife and stopped communicating. Another couple we know of physically separated over the issue of Torah. These and other similar situations are indeed heartbreaking and I'm not sure that I have answers, except to walk in love and humility. We must submit to the voice of the Spirit of God in each situation, remaining in constant prayer for the non-believing partner.

Sometimes the attacks against those growing in the direction of Torah observance will come from their own Christian brothers and sisters. I love the answer that Daniel Botkin gave to a brother who criticized his being 'under the law'.

A reader sent the editor of Gates of Eden three pages of quotes from Paul's epistles and ended with, *"If keeping the law makes you a better Christian - go for it. But you shouldn't judge those who don't, because we are not under the law of Moses but under the law of love for God and each other."*

I enjoyed Dr. Botkin's response:

> *"Please understand this: You keep the law too, brother. You keep 9 of the 10 commandments. There are also other Old Testament commands that you keep. It's not an issue of keeping or not keeping the law, because you and I both keep the law. You keep those parts of the law that you believe are still valid. The only difference between you and me is this: I happen to believe that Sabbaths and dietary laws are still valid; you don't. I'm no more 'under the law' than you are."* -DB [9]

Harmony of Law and Grace

To many, the Torah is seen as something opposed to grace. But nothing could be further from the truth. The Torah is an expression of God's grace; and it is His Spirit, which enables us to carry out the Torah in a way pleasing to Him. The Torah without the Spirit is death and the Spirit without the Torah is deception. Those who exclusively follow Torah need a revelation of God's Spirit, to remove their hearts of stone and replace them with hearts of flesh. Those who exclusively follow the Spirit, need a revelation of Torah, to place their feet back upon the solid footing of the 'Rock', the foundation, which is the Word of God. If we could only walk in both Spirit and Torah, a harmony of law and grace, perhaps we would see again the power and anointing of the first apostles, who walked with signs, wonders, and miracles.

---

9 *Ibid.* Botkin, (Nov-Dec. 2000, Vol. 6 No. 6)

Worshipping in Spirit and in Truth

One who is a true worshipper of God will worship Him in both Spirit and in truth. He or she is doubly sealed – with both the Torah and the Holy Spirit. Isaiah said,

> **"Bind up the testimony, and seal the Torah among my disciples."** (Is. 8:16)

We are warned not to grieve the Holy Spirit,

> **"...whereby you are sealed unto the day of redemption."** (Eph. 4:30)

Spirit Filled, Torah observant Believers are double sealed!

Torah is not Enough

As I was writing this book, I had a growing sense of uneasiness. I knew that what I was writing was correct – that we need to grow and mature in obedience to the Torah, but I also had the sense that I was missing something very important – vital in fact, to the life of the believer. This is the Holy Spirit. Although this book emphasizes the need to re-discover the beauty and value of the Torah, if this is the only aspect of our life in God that it encourages then I have failed. For I am going to make a statement that may astound some Torah observant believers. Torah is not enough. In fact, if Torah is kept in the flesh, it will bring death.

> **"For the letter kills, but the Spirit gives life."** (2 Cor. 3:6)

We need to experience the Ruach HaKodesh, the Spirit

of God, in our lives. After all, if the Torah was enough, why would Yeshua have instructed his disciples not to leave Jerusalem on their great commission, but rather to wait for the promised Spirit?

> **"And being assembled together with them, He commanded them not to depart from Jerusalem, but to wait for the Promise of the Father, which, He said, 'You have heard from Me. For John truly baptized with water, but you shall be baptized with the Holy Spirit not many days from now.'"**
> (Acts 1:4, 5)

The disciples of Yeshua, even though they were the ones who physically sat in His presence and under His teachings, were incapable of fulfilling their God-given assignment until the Holy Spirit had empowered them for the task.

> **"But you shall receive power when the Holy Spirit has come upon you; and you shall be witnesses to Me in Jerusalem, and in all Judea and Samaria, and to the ends of the earth."** (Acts 1:8)

Called But Impotent?

Do you feel called, but impotent, incapable, and powerless to complete the task? Don't lose heart! There is good news. Yeshua promised not to leave us as orphans but to send us the Holy Spirit who would be our helper. In Hebrew, He is called our comforter. We only need to ask for His help and comfort daily. We enter now into an intimate relationship with God through a new and living way. The veil separating

us from the very throne of God has been torn. When Yeshua
died, it was torn in half, opening the way for us to come into
His presence boldly, but only sprinkled in the blood of the
Lamb of God. Through the blood of Yeshua we may enter
into the Holy of Holies.

We are, at this time, preparing for an apostolic mission
to the nations. God has called us and is sending us out of the
Land of Israel, as is our primary mission – to be a light unto
the nations. I was sitting weeping, confessing my complete
lack of qualifications, lack of capabilities, lack of 'whatever
it's gonna take' to do this thing. What will I speak to all these
people? How will I cope with all the demands of travelling
with the children? Questions and doubts flooded my mind.
Above my desk is a sign that someone sent me which spoke
to my heart. It reads, *"God doesn't call the qualified. He
qualifies the called."*

Remember Moses? And God still said, *"Go!"* It is only
when we feel that we have no qualifications in ourselves
to do Him any good whatsoever that He can begin to use.
We then know that it is Him in us and through us and not
us in ourselves. We are only the broken vessels. He is the
potter and we are the clay. It seems that He must continually
remind us of this sobering and humbling truth. He uses not
the great, the powerful, the spiritual, the wise and wonderful
of this world, but the foolish and the weak. So that we may
not glory in ourselves, but let the weak say 'I am strong' and
the poor say 'I am rich', because of Him. It's all because of
Him.

Entering Into The Holy of Holies

And so, although I had prayed to be filled with the Holy Spirit many years ago, and could talk in tongues with the best of the charismatics, I knew that I needed more. I needed to enter into His very presence. Sitting there, I prayed a simple prayer of faith, which I invite you to pray as well. I believe you will actually experience, as I did, the peace and rest of entering into the presence of God in the most holy of places, the Holy of Holies. Here only the High Priest, the Cohen HaGadol could enter – and even he only once a year on the Day of Atonement (Yom Kippur), and only after the sacrifice had been performed with the utmost level of purity. What a privilege we have of drawing near to God, but we may do so only through the High Priest Himself, who is our Saviour, Yeshua.

> **"Therefore brethren, having boldness to enter the Holiest by the blood of Yeshua, by a new and living way which He consecrated for us, through the veil, that is His flesh, and having a High Priest (Cohen HaGadol) over the house of God, let us draw near with a true heart in full assurance of faith..."** (Heb. 10:19-22)

> **"Let us therefore draw near with confidence to the throne of grace, that we may receive mercy and may find grace to help in time of need."** (Heb. 4:16)

Here is the prayer I prayed:

> "By faith in the blood of Yeshua, and the veil that was rent by His flesh, I draw near with a true heart of faith, and I confess that

right now, in Yeshua's name, without any
acknowledgement of qualification in myself,
I do enter into the holiest place of all by the
blood of Yeshua." [10]

I may add that I immediately added a quick, *"and please
don't kill me"* at the end. For I know that had the Cohen
HaGadol not performed his duties properly, God would have
killed him on the spot. This same God that I was seeking,
is the God who struck down Uzza in an instant for touching
the ark presumptuously, for handling the holy things of God
in an improper way. And so it was not without fear that
I approached God in this way, trusting only in the blood
covering of His beloved Son.

I love a video we received from our children here in
Israel, which shows a depiction of Queen Esther's approach
to the king. In this film, she expresses real feelings – those
we don't usually think of when reading the scriptures. She
confessed her fear of approaching the throne of the king. If
he hadn't held out his golden sceptre, she would have been
put to death. But too much depended on her - the lives of
her people. And you know the happy ending to the Book
of Esther. Perhaps because of watching this video a zillion
times with my eighteen-month-old daughter, when entering
the Holy of Holies, I 'saw' myself bowing before the King
of Kings, and in relief knowing that He held out His golden
scepter to receive me with love. What peace security, and
comfort! For all those who have experienced rejection in
their lives (and who hasn't?), but especially for those who
have been rejected by their earthly fathers, it is my hope and
prayer that you will enter into this place of intimacy, love,
and acceptance with your Heavenly Father. For all those
who enter sprinkled with the blood of His Son, Yeshua, will
find complete acceptance in His arms.

---

10 Art Katz, *'Apostolic Foundations, The Challenge of Living an
Authentic Christian Life'*, pg. 46

The Spirit Brings Life

According to Scripture it is the Spirit of God that brings life when we obey Him in truth.

"Then those who received his word were baptized; and that day about three thousand souls were added to them." (Acts 2:41)

On Mt. Sinai, three thousand died due to their failure to keep even the minimal requirements of the Ten Commandments that had just been given to them. They had just said, *"All that the Lord has said we will do"*, and a few days later had broken their promise, fashioning for themselves an idol to worship, a golden calf. The Torah without the Spirit will bring death. The Spirit with the Torah brings life.

I don't want to speak to you from words, or pet doctrines, but out of the experience of learning and growing in the Lord. We are all in the process of growing and maturing in our relationship with the Lord. But even in our own family we have experienced this death that comes from trying to keep the Torah in the flesh. The Lord had to bring us to the place of crying out to Him when we think we're doing everything right and everything is going wrong. It is because we are trying to keep His Torah in our own flesh. It brings a hardness, a critical, religious spirit, a judgmental attitude towards others. Our hearts begin to turn back into stone without the Holy Spirit. We start to feel self-righteous and proud – that *we* are keeping Torah and *they* are not, therefore *we* are better than *they*!

This is a stench in God's nostrils and I see it at times in Torah observant believers. God says it is His Spirit which will compel us to keep His commandments (Ezek. 36:27). We are not to be driven into obedience out of pride so that we can flaunt our Torah observance in front of others. We are then no better than the Pharisees which Yeshua warned us about who grow lengthy beards and lengthen their tzitzit (fringes) just as a show for others to see. They 'doven' (pray) loudly and love to be called prestigious names and sit in the best seats in the congregation. There is nothing wrong with growing a beard or wearing tzitzit – but it is our heart's motive that counts. Is it out of love for God, or a desire for significance, identity, and recognition by men?

Loving One Another

Daniel Botkin also deals with an essential element of our faith in his article, "Loving One Another".[11]   Some people become so involved in their quest to become Torah observant that they neglect one of the two greatest commandments, according to Yeshua: to love one another. (Matt. 22:3540) Some Messianic believers may learn to speak (or better yet, chant) all the Hebrew blessings and prayers fluently, dance the Hebraic dances, keep all the Feasts of the Lord, observe dietary kashrut, and understand all the deep mysteries of the Torah. But if we have not love, then we are still nothing. (1 Cor. 13)

Here is a quote from the conclusion of his article that we would all be wise to heed,

> "If we cannot keep the Torah's great commandment to love one another, all of our other scrupulous, letter-perfect Torah

11   *Ibid.* Botkin, (Nov-Dec. 2000, Vol. 6 No. 6)

keeping will not give us spiritual life. It will only sink our roots deeper into death and serve as a witness against us on the Day of Judgment when our lack of love is exposed for all the world to see."

"We know that we have passed from death to life, because we love the brethren. He who does not love his brother abides in death. Whoever hates his brother is a murderer, and you know that no murderer has eternal life abiding in him."
(1 John 3:14, 15)

If we truly want to be living witnesses for Yeshua, then our greatest responsibility is to demonstrate love.

"By this all will know that you are My disciples, if you have love one for another"
(John 13:35)

If our Torah observance causes our love to grow cold or our hearts to grow hard, then we need to take a step back and ask ourselves what is wrong. We need to repent for grieving the Holy Spirit with our self-righteous religion.

One of the most tragic statements that I hear in Israel, is when people we share the gospel with say that they cannot put their faith in Yeshua as the Messiah because His followers murdered so many Jews. How this stumbling block to Jewish salvation could have been avoided if only Yeshua's followers had truly heeded His words about loving one another and avoiding religious hypocrisy. These so-called Christians allowed pride and arrogance to infect their spiritual walk with God and turn their hearts to stone, thereby robbing Jews of their faith in God as well as their

Messiah. This is truly the work of the one who steals, kills, and destroys. Yeshua said that the love of many would grow cold. Let us not allow this hardness or coldness to happen to us. We are not to be ignorant of the schemes of the enemy. (2 Cor. 2:11) We must allow the Holy Spirit to keep our hearts soft with His anointing oil. (2 Cor. 1:21, Ezek. 36:26, 27)

Christian festival seasons may be quite a struggle for some, especially those attempting to disentangle themselves from all remnants of paganism, the root of Babylon, and become more connected to their true biblical root - the God of Israel. It may be a prolonged time of wrestling with the issues involved, but I want to encourage you that if you persevere, you will prevail. Disassociating oneself from the well-accepted pagan aspects of our faith may not be easy, nor without pain.

Although in Israel Christmas passes almost unnoticed, in the Gentile nations Messianic believers likely encounter many who will disagree with them on the issue of Torah. Paul had a good word for Timothy that we may use as a guide. We are to avoid foolish and ignorant disputes that only generate strife.

"The servant of the Lord should not be quarrelsome, but gentle, patient, able to teach, in humility correcting those who are in opposition." (2 Tim. 2:23-25)

Filled With the Holy Spirit

The majority of Christians remember Pentecost as the time when God poured out His Holy Spirit upon the people as the Lord promised He would.

> "When the day of Shavuot had fully come,
> they were all with one accord in one place.
> And suddenly there came a sound from
> heaven, as of a rushing mighty wind, and
> it filled the whole house where they were
> sitting. Then there appeared to them
> divided tongues, as of fire, and one sat
> upon each of them. And they were all filled
> with the Holy Spirit and began to speak
> with other tongues, as the Spirit gave them
> utterance." (Acts 2:1-4)

When people call this the 'birth of the Church', I wonder
if they realize that these people were all either Jews or
proselytes (converts to Judaism). At this time, no evidence
had yet been presented that the good news of the gospel
applied to Gentiles. The Jewish foundation of the gospel
has largely been forgotten or ignored by a major portion of
the Christian Church. In this day however, God is moving
powerfully by His Holy Spirit to restore this awareness to
the Church.

CHAPTER THREE

THE PROPHETIC SIGNIFICANCE OF THE BOOK OF RUTH[12]

In both the portions of scripture, on Shavuot a two-fold command is given - to give an offering to the Lord, to thank him for His bountiful provision, and to care for the poor. The portion of scripture traditionally assigned to reading on Shavuot due to its occurrence at the time of the barley harvest is the book of Ruth. I believe that we, as people of God and especially as followers of Yeshua, can glean several prophetic truths from this Shavuot reading. Unfortunately, many Christians have been taught to almost disregard the Old Testament, and therefore miss much of the richness of their shared heritage in the God of Israel and the Jewish people. We held a Shavuot conference once at a retreat centre and stayed up late at night, reading and studying the book of Ruth, as is the tradition at the time of this feast. One woman, a devoted Christian for many years, was amazed! This was the first time she had ever read this portion of scripture. Considering that the Tanach (or 'Old Testament') was all that Yeshua and all his disciples considered the 'Word of

God', the Christian Church's reliance on the New Testament scriptures to the exclusion of the Tanach, the foundation of our faith, is truly tragic.

Naomi, wife of Elimelech, left the Promised Land to live for a time in the country of Moab. There, in exile, Naomi suffered the loss of most of her family – her husband and both her sons. As such, Naomi may represent grieving, bitter Israel – the many Jews who suffered persecution and hardship in the lands of their exile. Indeed, for many Jews of Eastern Europe, their entire families perished in the Holocaust. Some of the survivors have returned to the land of Israel, believing, as did Naomi,

> **"...that the Lord's hand has gone out against me."** (Ruth 1:13)

Naomi was bound through covenant, to two Gentile women, wives of her two dead sons. One was named Orpah and the other Ruth. Jews and Christians are also joined (whether they want to admit it or not) through covenant with the God of Israel and through the Messiah. The new covenant tells us that those who are 'Gentiles by birth', who used to be excluded from citizenship in Israel and foreigners to the covenants of the promise, without hope and without God in the world, are now included as fellow citizens with God's people and members of God's household (through the blood of the Jewish Messiah). (Eph. 2:1119) Therefore, Ruth and Orpah may represent two types of the Christian Church. Both are technically bound to Israel through covenant, but notice the two responses.

Orpah in Hebrew means 'back of the neck'. This daughter-in-law wept and kissed her mother-in-law goodbye before departing, at Naomi's insistence, to her own people and her own gods. There is a portion of the Christian Church, even that which professes love for Israel, which is only prepared to go so far with her. They are more comfortable with their own people and with their own paganized interpretation and worship of God. And yes, sometimes it is because the Jewish people push the well-meaning Christians away. But Ruth, whose name means 'friend or comrade', decided to stay with her widowed mother-in-law, despite her grief and her bitterness. Nothing could dissuade her from her complete devotion to Naomi. She clung to her, pleading,

> **"Don't urge me to leave you or to turn back from you. Where you go I will go, and where you stay I will stay. Your people will be my people and your God my God."**
> (Ruth 1:16)

Notice that Ruth pledged her allegiance to the people of Israel even before binding herself to the God of Israel. How many people today, who have bound themselves to the Lord through the Messiah, could claim the same? Here in the land of Israel, I personally know of several 'Ruths', both male and female. These are people, Gentiles by birth, aware of their intimate link with Israel and the Jewish people through covenant, who have pledged their utter devotion unto the end. They live here for no other reason than to stand with and bless the Jewish people, even through hardship and sacrifice. I know of others who do the same in many nations. There exists a faithful remnant who stand as 'watchmen on the walls'. Their mission is to

> **"...give God no rest until He establishes Jerusalem and makes her the praise of the earth."** (Is. 62:7)

The Spirit of God is planting a supernatural love in the hearts of many Christians for Israel and the Jewish people. If you are reading this booklet, you are probably one of them.

Halleluyah! Many others, though, who represent Orpah, need to become aware of the significance of their choice to 'kiss Naomi goodbye'.

When Naomi finally realized how determined Ruth was to go with her, she finally stopped urging her to leave. Jewish people may reject the offers of friendship from Christians due to fear and mistrust, but when they see the sincerity and determination of the Gentile Christian to love the Jewish people, their resistance may gradually melt away. Naomi lashes out, as do many Jewish people today, against God, believing that He has made their lives very bitter. Secular Israelis especially, who have been through so much war, terrorism and bloodshed, believe that God has afflicted them; that it is the Almighty who has brought so much misfortune upon them (Ruth 1:2021). It is the role of the Christians, those who know the Messiah and the Word of God, to bring comfort to His people (Is. 40:12).

Boaz, as kinsman-redeemer in the book of Ruth represents Yeshua our Redeemer. Boaz protects Ruth and makes sure she is provided for. When she asks why she, a foreigner, a Gentile, has found favour in Boaz's eyes, what does he reply?

> **"I've been told all about what you have done for your mother-in-law... May the Lord repay you for what you have done. <u>May you be richly rewarded by the Lord, the God of Israel, under whose wings you have come to take refuge.</u>"** (Ruth 2:1012)

Do not think that the Lord does not take notice of those who offer kindness, mercy, and comfort to the Jewish people (and those who do not). Read Matthew 25:31 to the end of the chapter to discern how the Lord separates the sheep and the goats in the final judgement. Who does He declare righteous and who is cursed and damned? In this portion of scripture, the Lord's selection depends upon what one has or has not done for the least of His brothers and sisters. In this context, when Yeshua walked on earth, He states His mission as only towards the **"lost sheep of the house of Israel"** (Matt. 15:24). Therefore, these brethren He refers to here are of Israel. Who were the only ones saved when Joshua and his men destroyed all of Jericho? It was Rahab and her family. Why? Certainly it was not due to her righteousness or morality – she was a prostitute. No, kindness was shown to her because she showed kindness to Israel by helping the spies to escape (Josh. 2:12). One's actions or apathy towards Israel may become an exceedingly serious issue in the days to come.

Ruth asked Boaz, her kinsman-redeemer, to spread the corner of his garment over her (3:9). This seems like a lovely, romantic gesture, but unless we understand the original Hebrew text, we miss the spiritual significance of this episode. Ruth actually asks Boaz to take her under his wing, since he is her redeemer. This is an act of covenant.

In Ezekiel 16:8, the Lord says He spread His wing over the woman, thus entering into covenant with her.

"'I spread My wing over you and covered your nakedness. Yes, I swore an oath to you and entered into a covenant with you, and you became Mine,' says the Lord God."

Yes, those of us – Jew or Gentile – who have taken refuge under the mighty, protective wing of the Lord, our Redeemer, have become the special, treasured possession of God. It is all too easy to look upon our own nakedness and sin before the Lord, and forget His awesome, redeeming love. Even the people who have despised His oath and broken the covenant will be redeemed.

**"Yet I will remember the covenant I made
with you in the days of your youth, and I
will establish an everlasting covenant with
you."** (Ezek. 16:60)

Some people believe Israel to be lost and damned, but the Lord, Israel's redeemer, promises to make atonement for us and to bring Israel into an everlasting covenant of peace (Is. 54:7-10).

The story of Ruth ends happily ever after. Boaz marries Ruth and together, they give life to a son whom they named Obed. He was the father of Jesse, the father of David (Ruth 4:17). This union of Jewish Redeemer and devoted Gentile, produces a child in the lineage of King David and the Messiah of the world.

Naomi's womb was barren. She was unable to conceive new life.

**"But Naomi took the child, laid him in her
lap and cared for him. The women said,
'Naomi has a son.'"** (Ruth 4:16, 17)

Israel, in its present spiritual condition, is unable to conceive new life in her own womb. Bitter and grieving, survivors of exile, persecution, and the Holocaust, they say,

**"Our bones are dried up and our hope is
gone; we are cut off."** (Ezek. 37:11)

I sense in the people of Israel this heaviness, hopelessness, and spiritual oppression. But God has promised that these dry bones will live! First, He will bring the Jewish people back to the land of Israel. This He is doing – re-gathering the exiles of Israel from all four corners of the earth. But God also promises to put His Spirit in the people so that they will live and so that they will know Him.

> **"I will put My Spirit in you, and you shall live, and I will place you in your own land. Then you shall know that I, the Lord, have spoken it and performed it."** (Ezek. 37:14)

I believe that God is looking to and fro over the earth for a Ruth – for the Gentile devoted to the God and people of Israel – in order to give birth to new life and lay it in the lap of tired, worn-out Israel. This can only be accomplished through fervent intercessory prayer for the spiritual restoration of the nation of Israel. Will you answer the call of God to this noble and privileged position?

Replacement Theology

Unfortunately some of Christian churches believe in a false theology *"Because of the rejection of Christ, God has rejected the Jewish people and has broken His covenant with them - they are no longer the children of God. Now we, the Church, are God's people; we inherit all the blessings and promises, and the Jews inherit all the curses."* This theology totally contradicts the word of God who said through the prophet Jeremiah:

> **"This is what the Lord says: 'Only if the heavens above can be measured and the foundations of the earth below be searched out will I reject all the descendants of Israel because of all they have done,' declares the Lord."** (Jer. 31:37)

God is a covenant - keeping God, not like us, His wandering sheep:

> **"I will not violate My covenant nor alter what My lips have uttered."** (Ps. 89:34)

The book of Hosea is a picture of the Lord's love and faithfulness to His people who commit spiritual adultery:

> **"I will betroth you to Me forever; I will betroth you in righteousness and justice, in love and compassion. I will betroth you in faithfulness, and you will acknowledge the Lord."** (Hos. 2:19, 20)

The Lord asks,

> **"Where is your mother's certificate of divorce?"** (Is. 50:1)

In other words, *"Where is the 'get'?"* A Jewish woman whose husband divorces her requires a document called a 'get' in order to finalize the separation. Without this 'get' she is still considered married by the Rabbinate, and is not allowed to re-marry. My own sister spent a great deal of time, money and effort to secure a 'get' from her ex-husband in order to validate her re-marriage by Jewish law. God is, in essence, saying, *"Does anyone see this get? Was my arm too short to redeem you?"* Since the get does not exist, the separation between God and His Jewish people cannot be legally finalized. The door is open for complete reconciliation and restoration.

Times of the Gentiles Fulfilled

Paul asks,

> **"Did God reject his people? By no means!
> I am an Israelite myself, a descendant of
> Abraham, from the tribe of Benjamin.
> <u>God did not reject his people</u>, whom he
> foreknew."**   (Rom. 11:12)

Paul warns the Gentiles not to be ignorant about Israel
and to guard against pride:

> **"I do not want you to be ignorant of this
> mystery, brothers, so that you may not
> be conceited: Israel has experienced a
> hardening in part until the full number of
> the Gentiles has come in."**   (Rom. 11:25)

Luke also mentions this 'time of the Gentiles' being
fulfilled.

> **"Jerusalem will be trampled on by the
> Gentiles until the times of the Gentiles are
> fulfilled."** (Luke 21:24)

This miraculous event transpired in 1967, when Israeli
soldiers reached the remaining wall of the Temple and
recovered Jerusalem. This scripture says that when Jerusalem
is no longer trampled on by Gentiles (when it is back under
Jewish control), the times of the Gentiles are fulfilled. This
happened in our lifetime! Isn't that awesome, that the Lord
is fulfilling scripture right before our very eyes? We are such
a privileged generation to witness the mighty miracles that
God is working. But many Christians are missing it! Why?
Because of an attitude, all too prevalent, that says, *"I am*

a Christian; that is Israel; what does that have to do with me?"

God has a plan, and that plan centers on His home, Jerusalem, His local address.

> **"And so all Israel will be saved, as it is written: 'The Deliverer will come from Zion; He will turn godlessness away from Jacob. And this is My covenant with them when I take away their sins.'"** (Rom. 11:26, 27)

This temporary blindness that is upon most of Israel is absolutely necessary and within the great plan of God in order that salvation could come to the Gentiles. If the Jews had not 'rejected Christ' as some Christians say, then where would they be today? The Messiah instructed his disciples:

> **"Do not go among the Gentiles or enter any town of the Samaritans. Go rather to the lost sheep of Israel."** (Matt. 10:56)

Yeshua also resisted the plea of a Gentile woman for deliverance of her demon-possessed daughter. He said,

> **"I was sent only to the lost sheep of Israel."** (Matt. 15:24)

The prophet, Isaiah, knew through the Holy Spirit that the Messiah would bring salvation to all of mankind, not just to Israel.

> **"It is too small a thing for You to be My Servant to restore the tribes of Jacob and bring back those of Israel I have kept. I will also make You a light for the Gentiles,**

**that You may bring My salvation to the
ends of the earth.**" (Is. 49:6)

Yeshua knew that the Gentiles would crucify Him, and
yet He loved them enough to die for them as well:

**"He will be handed over to the Gentiles.
They will mock Him, insult Him, spit on
Him, flog Him, and kill Him. On the third
day He will rise again.**" (Luke 18:32, 33)

So many Jewish people have been persecuted, deprived
of their human rights, exiled from their homes, tortured,
burned at the stake, and murdered for the sake of the label,
'Christ-killer'. Do you know how many people believe this
lie? The father of lies, the devil, has convinced many people
of this distortion of truth. Isn't it the ultimate irony to use
the people of the Messiah, adopted into the family of God
to persecute their own brothers and sisters in the very name
of the Messiah Himself? Using a Greek substitute, 'Jesus
Christ', they have succeeded in alienating the Jewish people
from their very own Messiah, by masquerading him as an
anti-Semitic Gentile.

And yet, there is nothing that can stand in the way of the
plans and purposes of the Lord! Just as Joseph's brothers
did not recognize him in Egypt since he was dressed in
Egyptian garb, once he revealed himself with the words,
"Ani Yosef" (I am Joseph), his brothers wept in repentance.
Joseph extended his love and forgiveness to his brothers and
they were reconciled forever. Isn't this a beautiful picture of
how the Lord will reveal himself to His Jewish brothers and
sisters?

**"They will look on Me, the one they have
pierced, and they will mourn for Him as**

**one mourns for an only child, and grieve
bitterly for Him as one grieves for a
firstborn son."** (Zech. 12:10)

The Jewish people will finally see Him, not as an
'Egyptian', a'Gentile', but as their Jewish brother. I believe
He will say to them, as Joseph said to his brothers,

**"And now, do not be distressed and do not
be angry with yourselves for selling me
here, because it was to save lives that God
sent me ahead of you."** (Gen. 45:5)

What a picture of grace – not only did he forgive, but he
encouraged them not to be overly sorrowful, because it was
within God's plan that he suffer so that many lives could be
saved. So did the Messiah suffer, to save the whole world. It
is not God's will that even one should perish. The Lord said
that He willingly laid down His life for His sheep, and that
no one, not Jew nor Gentile, took it from Him.

**"I am the good shepherd... The reason My
Father loves Me is that I lay down My life
– only to take it up again. No one takes
it from Me, but I lay it down of My own
accord. I have authority to lay it down and
authority to take it up again."** (John 10:14-
18)

Isn't it time to end the name-calling? Believing that
the Jews rejected and killed Christ is a lie, and its fruit is
hatred and death. Remember that when the Lord rode into
Jerusalem on the colt of a donkey, all those people who
shouted *"Hosanna"* and waved palm branches were not
Christians; they were Jews. God is restoring the Messiah
to the Jewish people; and if it is of God, nothing can stop it!

More Jewish people have come to receive Yeshua as their Messiah since 1967, than in all the years previously. It is God's appointed time; Jerusalem is in the hands of the Jewish people; the times of the Gentiles are fulfilled; the nation of Israel is re-born and the desert is blooming.

Role of Gentile Believers
– No Longer Foreigners

The Messiah came to break down the dividing wall of hostility that separates Jews and Gentiles. That wall that so-called 'Christians' re-built with Jewish blood from the Crusades, the Spanish Inquisition, the Russian pogroms, and the Holocaust, (all atrocities done in the name of Christ), is coming down brick by brick. Some Christian leaders are urging churches around the world to repent for the sins of the Christian Church against the Jewish people. Christians are travelling to Europe, and then to Israel retracing the very steps of the Crusaders, their tears of repentance washing away the stains of Jewish blood on the very ground they tread.

If Christians do not repent for the sins of their forefathers, who will? God has said,

> **"If My people, who are called by My name, humble themselves and pray, and seek My face and turn from their wicked ways, then will I hear from heaven and will forgive their sin and will heal their land."**
> (2 Chron. 7:14)

I believe that God is calling Christians to join together in repentance for sins committed against the Jewish people, and to bless them. God promised Abraham and his descendants:

"I will bless those who bless you, and whoever curses you I will curse."
(Gen. 12:3)

God has proved this word true throughout human history – from Pharaoh and Egypt to Haman in the book of Esther, to Germany and the Holocaust.

"...for whoever touches you touches the apple of His eye." (Zech. 2:8)

If the church has cursed the Jews, then they need to do whatever is in their power to bless them.

"For if the Gentiles have shared in the Jews' spiritual blessings, they owe it to the Jews to share with them their material blessings." (Rom. 15:27)

Many more Jews need to return to the land of Israel, since anti-Semitism is on a dangerous climb, and may continue to do so if and when the economies of the nations fail. Recently, three synagogues were bombed in the United States, and Orthodox Jews walking home from synagogue were shot at by a gunman from the 'Worldwide Church of the Creator'. Will someone please explain to me how people who call themselves Christians, followers of a Jewish Messiah, can be such virulent haters of Jews?   Isaiah tells us that Gentiles will help bring the Jewish people home where they will be safe from the Pharaohs, Hamans, and Hitlers of the world.

"See, I will beckon to the Gentiles, I will lift up my banner to the peoples; they will bring your sons in their arms and carry your daughters on their shoulders."
(Is. 49:22)

Gentile Christians play a significant role in God's end-time plan, but they must first enlarge their vision to see what God is doing beyond their own church, denomination, or city.

God promised to love those who were not originally His covenant people, those who are not of the nation of Israel, the Gentiles:

> **"I will show My love to the one I called 'Not My loved one'. I will say to those called 'Not My people', 'You are My people', and they will say, 'You are my God.'"** (Hos. 2:23)

People who are Gentile by birth are brought into covenant with the God of Israel through the blood of His Messiah and become part of, but do not replace, the people of Israel:

> **"Therefore, remember that formerly you who are Gentiles by birth and called 'uncircumcised' by those who call themselves 'the circumcision'... remember that at that time you were separate from the Messiah, excluded from citizenship in Israel and foreigners to the covenants of the promise, without hope and without God in the world. But now in Messiah Yeshua you who once were far away have been brought near through the blood of Messiah. For He Himself is our peace, who has made the two one and has destroyed the barrier, the dividing wall of hostility... For through Him we both have access to the Father by one Spirit. Consequently, you are <u>no longer foreigners and aliens</u>, but fellow citizens with God's people and members of God's household."** (Eph. 2:11-19)

Are you getting a clearer picture of God's love and faithfulness to both His first covenant people, Israel, and also to those who join the family, through the Messiah, by God's grace? Paul says that Gentiles are 'grafted in' amongst the branches of the olive shoot and *share* in the nourishing sap of its root. Paul again warns the Gentiles not to become arrogant and think that they support the root, when the root supports them. (Rom. 11:1718). Has the Christian Church cut itself off from its Jewish root and attached itself to a Greek/Roman/Babylonian root, which is pagan and unholy?

Understanding the Jewishness of the Gospel

At the time Messiah lived, the Jewish people were filled with Messianic expectation; they were looking for a deliverer to restore the kingdom of Israel from Roman rule. But Yeshua could not accept the role of conquering king at this time, for He knew that He must first die as the Passover lamb. When the Lord returns and places His feet on the Mount of Olives, He will not return as the meek, sacrificial lamb, but as the warrior Lion of Judah, to execute judgement on all the wicked, and on all nations who attacked Jerusalem. Israel will recognize their Messiah and experience a national, spiritual revival in the land:

> **"I am going to make Jerusalem a cup that sends all the surrounding peoples reeling... On that day, when all the nations of the earth are gathered against her, I will make Jerusalem an immovable rock for all the nations. All who try to move it will injure themselves... On that day I will set out to destroy all the nations that attack Jerusalem. And I will pour out on the house of David and the inhabitants of Jerusalem a spirit of grace and supplication."** (Zech. 12:2-3, 9-10)

The Lord will fight for Israel and all the saints will be with Him.

"Then the Lord my God will come, and all the holy ones with Him." (Zech. 14:5)

Where will the saints be who have ignored and slandered or even hated the people of Israel?

In one of my church presentations for their children's ministry, out of over one hundred children learning about Passover, not one knew that the Lord will return to Jerusalem. They all thought He was coming back to the United States or Canada. Why? Because their parents have not taught them important truths about God's relationship with Israel and the Jewish people, and how Christians are grafted into this Biblical faith of our Messiah. This is because most Christian Churches have ignored the Jewish roots of their faith, to their own detriment.

Understanding the Jewishness of the gospel is a key to a richer and deeper faith in God and the Messiah. I have been deeply touched to see even pastors, as well as their congregations, weeping when they finally comprehend their faith through Jewish eyes. In Passover, (Pesach), they see Yeshua as the Passover lamb. In the Feast of Firstfruits (Bikkurim), they see Him offered up to the Father as the firstfruits of those who will rise from the dead, the resurrection. In the Feast of Tabernacles (Sukkot), they see Him as Immanu-El (in Hebrew translated as 'With us – God'), the child born of a Jewish virgin, named Miryam, the miracle of God stooping down to dwell (tabernacle) with His people.

The Gift of the Holy Spirit

Shavuot is one of the three pilgrim festivals; the other two are Passover and Feast of Tabernacles. At this time, many Jews from all nations gathered in Jerusalem.

Yeshua had instructed his disciples:

> **"Do not leave Jerusalem, but wait for the gift My Father promised, which you have heard Me speak about. For John baptized with water, but in a few days you will be baptized with the Holy Spirit."** (Acts 1:4, 5)

The people asked Yeshua if he would restore the kingdom to Israel at that time. People who believe that the Jews rejected Christ are wrong. The Jewish people desperately wanted Him to be their Messiah, to restore the Kingdom of Israel. So many people loved and followed Him, that those evil men who plotted His death could not arrest Him during the Feast of Passover or there would have been a riot! Yeshua replied to their questioning:

> **"It is not for you to know the times or dates the Father has set by His own authority. But you will receive power when the Holy Spirit comes on you; and you will be My witnesses in Jerusalem, and in all Judea and Samaria, and to the ends of the earth."** (Acts 1:7, 8)

The purpose of Shavuot, as the giving of the Holy Spirit, was to anoint people to be witnesses for the Messiah. Most people consider 'Pentecost' the birth of the 'church', but it was not the birth of the Christian church as we know it today. At Shavuot, the Holy Spirit fell upon the Jewish believers, and God-fearing Jews from every nation heard them speaking in their own language and were amazed. (Acts 2:18) Peter addressed the large crowd of Jews gathered in Jerusalem for Shavuot and three thousand accepted his message and were immersed. Ritual immersion (or mikvah) was and still is a common ritual cleansing custom. It is used by women as part of married life, and is also used as the last step in converting a Gentile to a Jew. Its purpose is to cleanse from sin or impurity. This is the Jewish root of 'baptism', which is another Greek import.

Some Christians, in error, believe that 'Pentecost', the supposed birth of the Christian Church, was the first time that the Spirit of God fell upon God's people. I have heard Christians express amazement that they actually sensed the presence of the Holy Spirit upon a Jew who doesn't know Yeshua as the Messiah! But the Old Testament is full of examples of visitations of the Holy Spirit upon people. In one instance, Samson demonstrated incredible strength when the Spirit of God came upon him. In another, Saul was changed into a completely new man when the Spirit of the Lord fell. King David pleaded with God,

"Take not Thy Holy Spirit from me."
(Ps. 51:11)

What is at the root of this Christian attitude that they alone, the Church, could possibly be filled with the Holy Spirit and know God? I believe it is the same pride that Paul warned against.

"Do not boast against the branches. But if you do boast, remember that you do not support the root, but the root supports you." (Rom. 11:18)

CHAPTER FOUR

ANTI-TORAH ATTITUDES DOES GRACE NULLIFY THE LAW?

Three thousand lives were saved on Shavuot when the Lord gave us His Holy Spirit, but three thousand lives were lost on Shavuot at Mount Sinai due to the people's disobedience and idolatry when the Lord gave us His commandments. Therefore, a common Christian view is that 'the law brings death'. Most Christians seem to hold a negative view of 'the law', claiming to be not under law, but under grace. In fact, this verse explains that grace is what gives us the power to keep God's laws.

> **"For <u>sin shall not be your master</u> because you are not under law, but under grace."** (Rom. 6:14)

People of the Messiah need not stay in bondage to sin, because we have been redeemed. Just as God sent a deliverer, Moses, to free the Israelites from the Pharaoh of Egypt and physical slavery, so has God sent a Redeemer, His own right arm, to free people from slavery to the Pharaoh of this world.

> **"But God demonstrates His own love for us in this: While we were still sinners, the Messiah died for us."** (Rom. 5:8)

Does grace give us license to break God's commandments and sin against Him?

> **"What then? Shall we sin because we are not under law but under grace? By no means!"** (Rom. 6:15)

Instead of slavery to sin, we are now slaves to righteousness. This is good news!

> **"But now that you have been set free from sin and have become slaves to God, the benefit you reap leads to holiness, and the result is eternal life."** (Rom. 6:22)

I'm afraid that the prevailing notion among most Christian communities is that 'Christ has set us free from the law!' Paul asks,

> **"Is God the God of Jews only? Is He not the God of Gentiles too? Yes, of Gentiles too, since there is only one God, who will justify the circumcised by faith and the uncircumcised through that same faith. Do we, then, nullify the law by this faith?"**

And he answers his own question,

> **"Not at all! Rather, we uphold the law."** (Rom. 3:2931)

The Messiah has set us free indeed, but it is freedom from

sin, from breaking God's laws, not from the commandments themselves.

Is The Torah Abolished?

It seems, from a Jewish point of view, that most Christians pride themselves on somehow being 'above the law of God', not restricted as are Jews by dietary laws, Sabbath keeping, and other commandments. Paul said that:

> **"The law is holy, and the commandment is holy, righteous and good."** (Rom. 7:12)

God gave the nation of Israel the Ten Commandments, inscribed by the very finger of God (Deut. 9:10), but this does not mean they remain the exclusive possession of this one nation. This foundation of a moral and just life, pleasing in the eyes of God, applies to every person on earth, Jew or Gentile. God gave His commandments first to the Jew, just as He also gave His Word and His Messiah first to the Jew, but they are equally for the Gentile through covenant with the God of Israel. Israel's mission has always been to be a light to the nations, the goyim – to teach Gentiles the ways of God.

> *"The Ten Commandments, the heart of God's law, are just as applicable today as they were 3,000 years ago because they proclaim a life-style endorsed by God. They are the perfect expression of who God is and how He wants people to live."*

We could focus on the prevailing Christian tendency to break the second and fourth commandments regarding graven images and the seventh day Sabbath, but what about the other laws?

"God never issued a law that didn't have a purpose"

Some of the laws in the Tanach are specific to that time and culture, but the principles behind them remain valid. I do not believe that people's blatant disregard of His laws and commandments is pleasing in His sight. He told us that they are for our own good.

> **"And now, O Israel, what does the Lord your God ask of you but to fear the Lord your God, to walk in all His ways, to love Him to serve the Lord your God with all your heart and with all your soul, and to observe the Lord's commands and decrees that I am giving you today <u>for your own good?</u>"** (Deut. 10:12, 13)

Keep in mind, we are not here discussing man-made rules and laws imposed upon us by human authority such as, 'Do not play cards, do not dance, do not drink wine, do not mix dairy products with meat at the same meal, etc.'. We are talking about commandments decreed by God Almighty, Creator of the Universe, Lord of Lords and King of Kings. How dare we think that we are above His Word! Even Satan, the adversary, only wanted to be equal with God, but we in our pride and arrogance think we are somehow above His holy Word – that we can disregard it forever and suffer no consequence. If we may stop to learn a lesson from the Israelites, we can see the reason for God's hand of judgement upon them. Why was the land made desolate and the people sent into a terrible exile where many suffered and perished at the hands of the goyim? Jeremiah gives us the answer.

> "It is because they have forsaken My law, which I set before them, they have not obeyed Me or followed My law. Instead, they have followed the stubbornness of their hearts." (Jer. 9:13, 14)

Isaiah also gives us an understanding of the reason for God's anger against His people:

> "...for they have rejected the law (Torah) of the Lord Almighty and spurned the Word of the Holy One of Israel. Therefore the Lord's anger burns against His people." (Is. 5:24, 25)

We are all concerned for the welfare of our children, especially today in this evil and perverse generation. We desperately need the Lord to watch over these children of ours, subject to so much demonic influence in schools, television, music, videos, etc. But the Word says that if we ignore the Torah (law) of God, then He will also ignore our children:

> "Because you have rejected knowledge, I also reject you as My priests; because you have ignored the law of your God, I also will ignore your children." (Hos. 4:6)

Why is the earth under a curse today and in grave danger of complete destruction? Isaiah gives us the answer:

> "The earth is defiled by its people; they have disobeyed the laws, violated the statutes and broken the everlasting covenant. Therefore a curse consumes the earth; its people must bear their guilt.

**Therefore earth's inhabitants are burned
up, and very few are left."** (Is. 24:56)

From the perspective of God's Word, it seems as if the
majority of Christians have taken the bait of Satan in believing
a lie. The serpent has hissed into the ears of those whose sin
nature does not naturally want to be 'restricted' by various
laws and commandments, *"Did God really say...?"* The true
people of God need to be living according to His Word and
His Spirit, which gives us the grace to keep His ways, and
not according to the world. If it seems inconceivable that
everyone in your church or community could be wrong, then
perhaps it would help to review the story of Noah. From
amongst all peoples on the face of the earth, he was the only
one righteous because he walked in the ways of God. These
days, we are told, are like the days of Noah – most people are
dangerously unaware of what is coming. It is life as usual –
and then the end will suddenly be upon us.

Someone may even be a devoted and active servant of
the Lord, but still sin in the aspect of disregarding the laws of
God. Jehu, King of Israel, pleased God by destroying Baal
worship in Israel.

> **"The Lord said to Jehu, 'Because you have
> done well in accomplishing what is right in
> My eyes and have done to the house of Ahab
> all I had in mind to do, your descendants
> will sit on the throne of Israel to the fourth
> generation."** (2 Kin. 10:30)

And yet, Jehu failed by not obeying God with all his
heart.

> **"Yet Jehu was not careful to keep the law
> of the Lord, the God of Israel, with all his
> heart."** (2 Kin. 10:31)

The Sh'ma – the Law on our Hearts

The foundational prayer of Judaism is The Sh'ma:

"Hear O Israel (Shema Yisrael): The Lord is our God, the Lord is one. Love the Lord your God with all your heart and with all your soul and with all your strength. These commandments that I give you today are to be upon your hearts. Impress them on your children. Talk about them when you sit at home and when you walk along the road, when you lie down and when you get up. Tie them as symbols on your hands and bind them on your foreheads. Write them on the doorframes of your houses and on your gates." (Deut. 6:4-9)

When Yeshua was asked, *"Of all the commandments, which is the most important?"* he replied by quoting the Sh'ma. The second was the commandment, also from the Tanach,

"Love your neighbor as yourself."
(Lev.19:18; Mark 12:28-31)

Not only are we to keep God's commandments ourselves, God gives us the responsibility of teaching them to our children as a daily, everyday learning process. These laws and commandments are to be upon our hearts. The crux of this whole matter of law and Torah for the Christian is, *"Do the laws and commandments of God carry over into the new covenant from the Mosaic covenant?"* The new covenant was originally given first to Israel and Judah, but is also clearly for the Gentile through the blood of the Messiah, Yeshua. The prophet Jeremiah, among others, prophesied the coming new covenant:

> **"'The time is coming', declares the Lord,
> when I will make a new covenant <u>with
> the house of Israel and with the house of
> Judah.</u>"** (Jer. 31:31)

What is the essence, or the characteristics of this new covenant?

> **"I will put My law in their minds and write
> it on their hearts. I will be their God, and
> they will be My people... For I will forgive
> their wickedness and will remember their
> sins no more"**   (Jer. 31:33, 34)

God promises us forgiveness of our sins, but what has happened to His law under the new covenant? It has been written on our hearts – transformed from rules chiseled into tablets of stone, to an engraving upon soft hearts of flesh. This is the transformation of the new covenant. It has been transferred from a mere external ritual to an inner expression of our love for God. What is love for God?

> **"This is love for God: to obey His
> commands. And His commands are not
> burdensome."** (1 John 5:3)

What benefits are promised to the person who keeps the law in his or her heart?

> **"The law of his God is in his heart; none of
> his steps shall slide."** (Ps. 37:31)

What negative promise is given to those who refuse to listen to the Torah of God?

> **"One who turns away his ear from hearing**
> **the law, even his prayer is an abomination."**
> (Prov. 28:9)

What does it mean that we carry God's law in our hearts? We say this phrase so glibly, but one day the Lord showed me with a word picture what this really means. Every weekday, my youngest son heads out the door for school, a heavy knapsack on his back, juice bottle in the side pocket and sandwich in the front. As he climbs the stairs, my heart as usual, takes a little leap, knowing that I must trust the Lord to watch over him when he is out of my sight. I think of the Israeli schools as a kind of 'lion's den', and I always pray that God will preserve my little boy, still so young and tender, and send angels to close the mouths of the lions that may seek to devour him. I always remain outside to watch him mount the long flight of stone steps because I know that at some point, he is going to turn around, say, *"Bye Mom, I love you"* and finally blow me a kiss before he disappears out of sight. I always reach out to scoop up his kiss and I pat my chest, blowing him a kiss in return, while he does the same, patting it firmly into his little chest. He and I both know that our kisses are safely stowed away in our hearts and that we love one another. This, the Lord showed me, is what it means to keep His law in our hearts. It means that even though we cannot see this God, we remember Him and we love Him always.

> **"This is love for God: to obey His**
> **commands. And His commands are not**
> **burdensome."** (1 John 5:3)

We don't obey God's commandments in order to win brownie points or to earn our salvation. This is a gift of God's grace, for none of us deserve it. But the way to express our love for God, to demonstrate our deep commitment and devotion to Him is by keeping His law in our hearts and walking in obedience to His commandments. Carrying His law in our hearts is an indication of our desire that His will, not ours, be done.

> **"I desire to do Your will, O my God. Your law is within my heart."** (Ps. 40:8)

Sealed with Blood

What does Yeshua the Messiah have to do with all of this? All of God's covenants required blood.

> **"This is why even the first covenant was not put into effect without blood. When Moses had proclaimed every commandment of the law to all the people, he took the blood of calves, together with water, scarlet wool and branches of hyssop, and sprinkled the scroll and all the people. He said, 'This is the blood of the covenant, which God has commanded you to keep'... In fact, the law requires that nearly everything be cleansed with blood, and without the shedding of blood there is no forgiveness."**
> (Heb. 9:18-22)[13]

The Abrahamic and the Mosaic covenants were both sealed with sacrificial blood. This new covenant, however, was not sealed with blood – that is, not until Yeshua gave His own life as the perfect kapparah (atonement) for our sins.

His blood was the sealing of the new covenant between

---

13   See also Leviticus 17:11

God and Israel, which was later extended to all people.

At the Passover Seder, Yeshua held up the third cup of wine, the cup of redemption and said,

> **"This is My blood of the covenant which is poured out for many."** (Mark 14:24)

He declared that He would not drink the fourth cup of wine – the cup of praise – until the day He drinks it in the kingdom of God. At that time, we will all celebrate the Seder together at the marriage supper of the Lamb and sing praises to God.

Sacrificial Law Fulfilled

Yeshua fulfilled the *sacrificial law* with his death:

> **"Day after day every cohen (priest) stands and performs his religious duties; again and again he offers the same sacrifices, which can never take away sins. But when this Cohen (Yeshua) had offered for all time one sacrifice for sins, He sat down at the right hand of God. Since that time He waits for His enemies to be made His footstool, because by one sacrifice He has made perfect forever those who are being made holy."** (Heb. 10:11-14)

The Messiah redeemed us from the *curse* of the law by becoming a curse for us (Gal. 3:13), but He did not magically set us free from the obligation to keep the commandments.

> "Do not think that I have come to abolish
> the law or the prophets; I have not come to
> abolish them but to fulfill them. I tell you
> the truth, until heaven and earth disappear,
> not the smallest letter, not the least stroke
> of a pen, will by any means disappear from
> the law until everything is accomplished.
> Anyone who breaks one of the least of
> these commandments and teaches others
> to do the same will be called least in the
> kingdom of heaven, but whoever practices
> and teaches these commands will be
> called great in the kingdom of heaven."
> (Matt. 5:17-19)

How many preachers of the Word of God are teaching
Gentile Christians that the law is abolished and therefore
they do not need to keep God's commandments – that we
are now under grace, not under law? I have actually heard
a pastor call the commandments of God *"crap, refuse, and
rubbish"*. Why, I asked him, if the commandments are no
longer valid, does the church spend hours exhorting people
to keep the commandment on tithing? It seems that the
church is getting a mixed message: on the one hand, we are
to lead holy, righteous lives to the best of our abilities and
not sin. On the other hand, we are not to concern ourselves
with keeping God's commandments, which point out what is
sin and what is not.

> "Blessed are they whose ways are
> blameless, who walk according to the law
> of the Lord. Blessed are they who keep
> His statutes and seek Him with all their
> heart... You have laid down precepts that
> are to be fully obeyed...Open my eyes that
> I may see wonderful things in Your law. I

**am a stranger on earth; do not hide Your
commands from me. My soul is consumed
with longing for Your laws at all times.
You rebuke the arrogant, who are cursed
and who stray from Your commands...
Your statutes are my delight; they are my
counselors."** (Ps. 119:1, 2, 4, 18-21, 24)

This is just a brief selection of verses from Psalm 119.
The commentary in my bible says,

*"Obedience to God's laws is the only way
to achieve real happiness. Most of us chafe
under rules, for we think they restrict us
from doing what we want... But God's laws
were given to free us to be all He wants us to
be. They restrict us from doing what might
cripple us and keep us from being our best.
God's guidelines help us follow His path and
avoid paths that lead to destruction."* [14]

I think that says it very well. The Torah is a 'law of
liberty'. It sets us free from sin. The Spirit of God gives us
the power to keep God's Torah.

Blessing or Cursing

Recently, at a Women's Aglow meeting where I was
speaking on the Jewish roots of the Christian faith, a woman
came up for prayer. She had been sick for some time and
was angry that her prayers for healing didn't seem to be
getting through. I felt the Lord telling me that this woman
was sick from eating unclean meats such as pork. I hesitated

---

14   NIV Life Application Bible

to give her this word, since the group had just finished eating bacon and eggs for breakfast, and I hate to be thought of as legalistic, or even worse, a Judaizer! Eventually, as I beat around the bush, this precious woman understood what I was trying to sensitively share with her, and she began to weep and thank me profusely. She had always felt convicted over eating pork, but her Christian friends had told her she was being 'religious'. She had eaten a large portion of ham over Easter and had been sick ever since. She actually thanked me for giving her permission to keep a commandment of God regarding our diets. Do we think that God does not care about what we put into our bodies? Does the Creator of these bodies not know what is fit for human consumption and what is not? Did He selfishly keep it a secret from us? No, He gave us the owner's manual. Did our digestive systems change when the Messiah died on the cross? People claim that we have better sanitation methods and refrigeration technology that now makes this meat acceptable and these Old Testament laws obsolete. Simply because we can now avail ourselves of condoms, does that render the laws against sexual immorality obsolete? God is God and He does not change. Yeshua is the same yesterday, today and forever.

"If anyone turns a deaf ear to the law, even his prayers are detestable." (Prov. 28:9)

Just like this woman who was not receiving healing, could this be a reason why so many Christians become frustrated by unanswered prayers? If someone breaks the law of gravity by jumping off a very tall building, they are probably (barring a miracle) going to go splat and severely injure themselves or die. This will likely happen, even if they love God and God loves them, and even if they pray on the way down. If a person gets sick and dies of cancer from eating foods that God has specifically warned us not to eat, then this is the consequence of disobedience to the law, not a reflection on God's love and grace.

Even in the nation of Israel, some Christians continue to defy or live in ignorance of God's laws. At a recent Russian Christian fellowship, I was surprised to find that someone had brought a crab and seafood salad to the pot luck. Now, in Israel, most stores do not sell unclean foods such as pork or seafood (Lev. 11, Deut. 14), but some of the Russian immigrants have managed to somehow import these. The irony of the situation was that I was made to feel that I must apologize for my refusal to eat the salad, as if I was indulging in the unpardonable sin of legalism. Not only this, but these people, all dedicated Christians, did not even know that God's Word forbids the eating of shellfish. One woman said to me, *"Well, what's wrong with it? It's all from the sea!"* I fear for these people who sin out of ignorance, since they have the Word of God right in front of them – in their hands! What will be their excuse before God?

Most of the Gentile Christian's turning away from God's commandments stems from the book of Acts.

Peter's Vision – People or Food?

In Acts chapter 10, Peter has his famous vision of the unclean (non-kosher) animals descending from heaven in a large sheet and a voice telling Peter to get up, kill, and eat. The majority of the Christian church has interpreted this vision to mean that the food laws have been abolished. Pork and shellfish are popular items at Christian meetings and functions. One church organized a pig roast for their congregation to get together and petition the Lord for revival. I wondered if the Lord would even attend, since He was and still is a Torah-observant Jew. Nowhere in scripture does He claim to change His faith; neither do His followers. Peter himself wondered about the meaning of the vision, since he had never eaten anything impure or unclean in his life and could not understand why the voice would ask him to do so. The voice spoke to Peter a second time saying,

> **"Do not call anything impure that God has made clean."** (Acts 10:15)

Finally Peter understood:

> **"You are well aware that it is against our law for a Jew to associate with a Gentile or visit him. But God has shown me that I should not call any impure or unclean."** (Acts 10:28)

Keep in mind that the reference to Gentile in scripture here is not to God-fearing people of the Bible, but to pagan, heathen, idol worshipping people who don't know the one true God. Prior to this time, the nation of Israel was commanded to keep themselves separate from the pagan people around them, lest they become ensnared by their ways. Intermarriage with Gentile wives proved the downfall of Israel, including king Solomon, as they were drawn into idolatry and worship of false gods. For Peter to claim that God now permits them to associate with and even eat with Gentiles was a radical idea that the Jewish believers resisted. Who could believe that Jesus is for the Gentiles?!

Peter understood the good news that the Messiah is for all people:

> **"I now realize how true it is that God does not show favoritism but accepts men from every nation who fear Him and do what is right."** (Acts 10:34, 35)

Still the Jewish believers resisted this radical idea. What finally convinced them was the Holy Spirit!

> **"While Peter was still speaking these words, the Holy Spirit came on all who heard the message. The circumcised believers who had come with Peter were astonished that the gift of the Holy Spirit had been poured out even on the Gentiles. For they heard them speaking in tongues and praising God."** (Acts 10:44-46)

Peter suffered much criticism for going into the house of uncircumcised men and eating with them, so Peter again explained the meaning of the vision – that he was not to consider these God-fearing Gentiles sent by Cornelius as unclean. When Peter testified that the Holy Spirit came on them as on the Jews at Shavuot,

> **"They had no further objections and praised God, saying, 'So then, God has granted even the Gentiles repentance unto life.'"** (Acts 11:18)

My point here is not to make non-Jewish believers feel like second class citizens in any way, shape, or form, but merely to demonstrate how very Jewish the gospel was at the time of the Messiah and how drastically the message has been changed by the traditions of man.

After this significant breakthrough, some of the Jews went to Antioch and began to speak to Greeks also, telling them about the good news of the Messiah.

"The Lord's hand was with them, and a great number of people believed and turned to the Lord." (Acts 11:20, 21)

So many Gentile people began to turn to the Lord, however, that issues began to crop up such as whether or not these Gentiles are required to become circumcised in order to follow the Messiah.

The Jerusalem Council

This matter was settled at the Jerusalem Council.

"It is my judgement, therefore, that we should not make it difficult for the Gentiles who are turning to God. Instead we should write to them, telling them to abstain from food polluted by idols, from sexual immorality, from the meat of strangled animals and from blood. For Moses has been preached in every city from the earliest times and is read in the synagogues on every Sabbath." (Acts 15:19-21)

I had always considered this a strange hodgepodge of restrictions on the Gentiles until I understood that these are not Bible-believing, God-fearing Christians, but people with absolutely no understanding of the ways of the Lord, people steeped in idol worship. All these prohibitions are practices associated with their worship of false gods and goddesses.

When we begin school, we do not start at university, but at kindergarten or even pre-school. If the teacher moves ahead in the lessons too quickly, we are likely to become frustrated and give up in despair. In the same way, these people, who had no knowledge of God, were to go to the synagogues every Sabbath, as did the Jewish believers. Here, the Gentiles would be discipled, since the commandments and laws of God would be preached each week. They were, however, expected to move progressively towards a Torah-observant, God-pleasing lifestyle by the leading of the Holy Spirit.

After all, do you see any prohibition in this passage against committing murder, stealing or lying? And yet, I am sure that most Christians would consider these transgressions as sin. Are Gentile Christians given license to dishonor their parents, steal, kill, or lie, simply because the decision at this council did not specifically forbid these? The argument that non-Jewish followers of the Messiah are not required to keep God's commandments because of this Jerusalem Council ruling does not hold up to logic. It is also insulting to non-Jews.

At a recent men's prayer meeting in Israel, one believer became absolutely furious at the suggestion that he should keep the Sabbath and not work on this day that God declared a day of rest. He proudly declared his right as a Christian, to work on the Sabbath or do anything he likes, since he is 'not under the law'. My husband asked him if he is also free to murder as well! Another believer became highly upset about the Sabbath and vehemently defended her 'Christian Sunday Sabbath', unaware of its root that comes straight from Babylon. This anger stems from a subtle anti-Semitism that proudly defends one's identity as a Christian, different and distinct from that of a Jew. This same woman claims to have been offered the right of citizenship in Israel if she would 'convert' to Judaism. She answered, "I would rather die first". Although I understand her intention is to declare her loyalty to 'Jesus', she forgets that Yeshua, himself was and still is a Jew. By insulting the Jews, she insults the Lord.

CHAPTER FIVE

ONE TORAH

The Word of God clearly states that there is to be only one standard, one set of rules and regulations, one Torah.

> **"One ordinance shall be for you of the assembly and for the stranger who dwells with you, an ordinance forever throughout your generations;... One Torah and one custom shall be for you and for the stranger who dwells with you."** (Num. 15:15, 16)

I find this notion of a separate, sub-standard set of rules for the Gentiles, arising out of what seems to me a misinterpretation of the decision of the Jerusalem Council (Acts 15), to be offensive towards non-Jews. Is the inference that for some reason, the Gentiles cannot handle the same standards of holiness, and therefore need only keep the four specifically mentioned regulations?

> **"Abstain from things offered to idols, from blood, from things strangled, and from sexual immorality."** (Acts 15:29)

If this were the case, then it seems perfectly acceptable, according to this interpretation, for Gentiles to go out and murder someone, dishonor their parents, or other assorted sins. Well, these are not mentioned among the four are they? Obviously, this is not the correct interpretation.

First of all, the people turning to God here, are not Bible believing, Gentile Christians. They are complete heathens; some translations say 'pagans'. To them the Torah is a completely unfamiliar, strange book. Granted, it is also to many of us saved out of the world, and we must start from square one too, whether we be Jewish or not.

Secondly, the decision of the Jerusalem Council centered upon the issue of circumcision – do non-Jews have to be circumcised before entering into the covenant? There was naturally quite a debate about this issue. Some rabbis said that the bris, the circumcision, was the most important issue, others said it was the mikvah, the water immersion. Obviously, this council decreed that circumcision was not a pre-requisite for turning to God and taking one's place in the covenants of promise. But there is an addition:

> **"For Moses has had throughout many generations those who preach him in every city, being read in the synagogues every Sabbath (Shabbat)."** (Acts 15:21)

What is this saying? It implies that these new converts are expected to join with Jewish worship and discipleship in the synagogues each Shabbat. In this way, they will gradually learn Torah and grow in their faith. By the way, for those who might be tempted to learn Torah in this way today, I'm afraid in most synagogues you would be sorely disappointed. For Moses and the Torah is not usually preached in practical sense there. I would suggest, that for those God is calling by His Spirit to learn more about Torah, to seek God for a discipleship program that is from Him.

There are, it seems, as many divisions and doctrines within the Messianic movement as there are within Christianity. And so it is 'buyer beware'. Be careful and seek the Lord's wisdom with whom to study. Of course, the Holy Spirit is the best teacher, along with the Word of God that He has so graciously provided us. We are promised not to be left as orphans, but to be given the Spirit of God who will lead and guide us into all truth. We need only be willing and open before the Lord to His guidance.

There is another sand trap that the enemy sets out for hapless believers to fall into when beginning a walk of submission to Torah. The enemy can use the new zeal of someone who suddenly 'discovers' Torah against them, by heaping condemnation if they don't change everything in their lives all at once, even though it takes time to learn how to keep Torah. It takes a lifetime. We cannot become harsh or impatient either with ourselves or others who don't 'get with the program' instantly. The following is my reply to a question a sister in the Lord sent me about her participation in the church's Easter egg hunt.

Dear Sister, I can sense in your letter that you are sincere and truly want to follow God and walk in His ways. But it's tough when it's such an upstream swim and all the other fish are swimming the other way, calling out to you, 'Hey! You're going the wrong wayyyyyy!!' My first impression was to tell you all about the paganism of Easter and send you some information and tell you that if you don't get out of Babylon you will be swept away with her sins (Rev. 18:4). But the Lord showed me something, I believe, that is in line with the decision of the Jerusalem Council in Acts 15. That is, we should not be too hard on Gentiles who are turning from paganism to God's ways and Torah. In the beginning, it can seem overwhelming. We must learn line by line and precept upon precept. Although we should all be moving in the direction of obedience to God's Word, it is difficult to change all at once everything in our lives. I would like to give the illustration through which God spoke to me:

Bowing in the House of Rimmon

Naaman, captain of the host of the King of Aram, was a mighty man but a leper. A little captive Jewish maid suggested he go to the prophet in Israel to find healing. He was instructed to wash seven times in the Jordan River to be cleansed of his leprosy. Naaman was angry. The rivers of Damascus, and other Gentile lands were far superior to Israel's Jordan River, he stated. But he was convinced to obey the prophet anyway and he came out of the river healed and cleansed, no longer leprous. Leprosy symbolized moral sin. The remedy for man's fallen moral condition is not found in the seemingly superior waters of India, Greece, Rome or any other land, but in the river of Hebraic, biblical teachings from the Torah. And because of his healing, Naaman dedicated himself to the God of Israel, knowing Him to be the one true God.

But then he asks the prophet's forgiveness (pardon).

> **"'In this thing the Lord pardon thy servant; when my master goes into the house of Rimmon to worship there, and he leans on my hand, I prostrate myself in the house of Rimmon. When I prostrate myself in the house of Rimmon, the Lord pardon thy servant in this thing.' And he (Elisha) said unto him, 'Go in peace'"**
> (2 Kin. 5:18, 19)

The phrase, 'to bow in the house of Rimmon', has

become an indication of unwilling homage, or dangerous compromise. Some would say that everyone should be like Daniel, and rather than compromise their faith, be thrown into the lions' den; or, like Shadrach, Meshach and Abednego, be thrown into the fire rather than compromise. But Naaman was a new believer, a baby in the faith as some would say. Elisha said, 'Go in peace.' He didn't say he approved, nor that he disapproved. I believe he was simply giving him leave and trusting the Lord to help him grow in faith and obedience. If Elisha had rebuked him for his 'bowing in the house of Rimmon', perhaps Naaman might have become discouraged and fallen away completely from his new turning to the one true God. And so I would also tend to say, 'Go in peace' and I trust that yes, one day you will have the strength and courage to take a stand.

Love Hannah

Only One Law

The Ten Commandments, written by the finger of God and given at Mount Sinai on Shavuot contain moral guidelines for all of mankind, not just the Jews. Those not born into the nation of Israel (called aliens or strangers) were always welcome to join the people of God – with one condition – they must live according to the laws of the land and leave behind those things which transgress the law. We spoke earlier about Gentiles in the Messiah being granted citizenship in the nation of Israel (Eph. 2:19).

When one becomes a citizen of Canada, for example, as did my husband when he immigrated from Poland, he was free to bring with him, from his country of origin, aspects of his culture and identity. For example, Radek still likes Polish food, manner of dress, familiar spices, etc. The new immigrant, however, must study and agree to abide by the laws of Canada. If someone happens to come from a country that practices cannibalism, for instance, this cannot be continued. The same law applies to Jew and Gentile alike who want to follow God.

> **"The community is to have the same rules for you and for the alien living among you; this is a lasting ordinance for the generations to come. You and the alien shall be the same before the Lord. The same laws and regulations will apply both to you and to the alien living among you."**
> (Num. 15:15, 16)

This instruction is repeated again:

> **"You are to have the same law for the alien and the native-born. I am the Lord your God."** (Lev. 24:22)

It seems to me that the Lord is making Himself perfectly clear. Gentiles are not native-born Jews, but through the blood of Messiah, they have been washed and cleansed from all paganism and must then live out this new life according to the ways of the Lord. Adopted children are fully accepted and equally loved as those naturally born, but both, I assume, will be expected to obey their father and abide by the rules and regulations of the home.

No, in the flesh we cannot do this. Our rebellious nature will remain at enmity with the law of God.

> **"The mind of sinful man is death, but the mind controlled by the Spirit is life and peace; the sinful mind is hostile to God. It does not submit to God's law, nor can it do so. Those controlled by the sinful nature**

**cannot please God. You, however, are
controlled not by the sinful nature but by
the Spirit, if the Spirit of God lives in you."**
(Rom. 8:6-9)

What controls you? Is it the sinful nature or the Spirit of
God? If we are truly controlled by the Spirit and if the Spirit
of God lives in us, we will submit to God's Laws.

The Sign of the Spirit: Obedience

With all this emphasis on the law, how does this fit
together with the Spirit, since Shavuot is a celebration of
both gifts? The prophet Ezekiel describes the promise of
the Spirit.

> **"I will sprinkle clean water on you, and
> you will be clean. I will cleanse you from
> all your impurities and from all your idols.
> <u>I will give you a new heart and put a new
> spirit in you</u>; I will remove from you your
> heart of stone and give you a heart of flesh.
> <u>And I will put my Spirit in you and move
> you to follow my decrees and be careful to
> keep my laws.</u>"** (Ezek. 36:25-27)

Note that the sign of God's Spirit dwelling within us is
our movement in the direction of obedience towards God's
laws. Many people believe that the sign of the Holy Spirit
is speaking in tongues. This, however, can be fabricated,
whereas obedience cannot!

Those who claim that this new heart and new Spirit is
only for Israel or the Jews, must also then say that Israel's
Bible and their Messiah and their God is theirs alone. This is

not true. Gentile Christians are not pagans or heathens, but share in the privilege and also the responsibility of Israel as a chosen, holy people.

> **"But you are a chosen people, a royal priesthood, a holy nation, a people belonging to God, that you may declare the praises of Him who called you out of darkness into His wonderful light. Once you were not a people, but now you are the people of God; once you had not received mercy, but now you have received mercy."** (1 Pet. 2:9, 10)

How, then, are we to live?

> **"But the day of the Lord will come like a thief. The heavens will disappear with a roar; the elements will be destroyed by fire, and the earth and everything in it will be laid bare. Since everything will be destroyed in this way, what kind of people ought you to be? You ought to live holy and godly lives."** (2 Pet. 3:10, 11)

Paul's Letters

I realize that the New Testament contains many scriptures that seem to contradict the Old Testament's view on 'the law'. Some claim that the law is useless, done away with, a snare and trap, something that Christians ought to beware of, lest they fall into it and become bewitched! However, we know that scriptures can be distorted and misinterpreted and even used by the enemy, as he used them against Yeshua in the desert. Peter wrote about Paul's letters,

> "His letters contain some things that are
> hard to understand, which ignorant and
> unstable people distort, as they do the
> other Scriptures, to their own destruction.
> Therefore, dear friends, since you already
> know this, be on your guard so that you
> may not be carried away by the error of
> lawless men and fall from your secure
> position." (2 Pet. 3:16, 17)

Do not lay the foundation of your faith in the words of
Paul, which I believe we are mistranslating and therefore
misinterpreting – to our own detriment. If our understanding
of Paul's words contradicts the Word of God in the Tanach,
then it is our comprehension of Paul's words that is incorrect,
not the Word of God.

Zealous for the Law

In this book we have already established that the Lord
Yeshua, all of His disciples, the apostle Paul and tens of
thousands of early believers were all zealous for the law
(Torah) of God. We are to follow their example and walk in
their footsteps.

> "We know that <u>we have come to know</u> <u>Him</u>
> <u>if we obey His commands.</u> The man who
> says, I know Him, but does not do what He
> commands is a liar, and the truth is not in
> him. <u>But if anyone obeys His Word, God's</u>
> <u>love is truly made complete in him.</u> This
> is how we know we are in Him: whoever
> claims to live in Him must walk as Yeshua
> did." (1 John 2:36)

To break God's commandments is to sin.

"No one who lives in Him keeps on sinning. No one who continues to sin has either seen Him or known Him." (1 John 3:6)

Before Yeshua died for our sins, keeping the law was a matter of obedience out of fear. Now we know that Yeshua paid the death penalty that we deserve for our sin, and that we have eternal life with God through the atonement of the Passover lamb. We strive to live a holy, righteous, and God-pleasing life, not to attain righteousness, but out of love and gratitude for what He has done for us. Living according to the commandments of God is our way of expressing our devotion and commitment to Him. Our objective is not to avoid punishment, or to earn some kind of spiritual brownie points, but to maintain a close relationship and to experience His blessing.

Mount Sinai – A Betrothal

The great event when God gave His people the Torah at Mount Sinai may be compared to a betrothal ceremony. God came to speak to His people in a thick cloud. God also led the people with a cloud by day. The cloud is the symbol of God's divine presence and guidance. (Ex. 13:21)

The cloud may also symbolize the covering of the 'chuppah', the marriage canopy, under which the Jewish bride enters into the covenant relationship of marriage with her bridegroom. What took place between God and Israel at Mount Sinai may be likened to a marriage ceremony. This took place, according to Jewish tradition, at Shavuot (Feast of Weeks or Pentecost). The conditions of the covenant were laid out and the responsibilities of each party clearly specified. In a Jewish wedding ceremony, these are written in the 'ketubah', the marriage contract. It states what the husband is responsible for in the marriage and also the wife, as well as what each may expect from the other. God clearly stated at Mt. Sinai His expectations of His bride, and what He is prepared to offer. Israel, His bride, said *"I do",*

"And all the people answered together, and said, 'All that the Lord hath spoken we will do.'" (Ex. 19:8)

Every bride is given a ring, a token, a sign that she is betrothed. What is the sign of betrothal God gave to Israel? It is the Shabbat. God said it will be a 'sign' between Him and the people of Israel; it is the wedding ring. I believe that the bridegroom also gave to His bride a wedding gift. This is the land of Israel, given as a promise to this special nation. Can we better consider the rage of the bridegroom towards those who attempt to take away His beloved's wedding gift?

An analogy may be made between our relationship with the Lord and with an earthly bridegroom. Because we love our betrothed, we try to do the things that please him – as an expression of our love. If my beloved had made clear what is pleasing in his eyes and I disregard this, instead doing whatever seems right in my own eyes, my fiancé would probably come to question the sincerity of my professed love. The marriage supper of the Lamb has not yet taken place – it is still to come – but some believers act as if the Lord is an old spouse one can take for granted. If my intended spouse has even written down what pleases Him and what is detestable in His sight, and I choose to read this document and then do the things which He hates, what message does this give to Him?

I remember once speaking at another Women's Aglow

meeting in which the praise and worship prior to the meeting was exceptionally beautiful. One song that struck me was a plea that we should love what God loves and hate what He hates. Inside, I thought how sad that these people sing this song in all sincerity, yet return from the lunch line-up with plates loaded high with ham and bacon, and set the plate down right next to the book that tells them this is detestable to God and not permissible for holy, chosen people.

Sh'ma Yisrael...

"Love the Lord your God and keep His requirements, His decrees, His laws and His commands always... Observe therefore all the commands I am giving you today, so that you may have the strength to go in and take over the land that you are crossing the Jordan to possess, and so that you may live long in the land...a land flowing with milk and honey... Fix these words of Mine in your hearts and minds; tie them as symbols on your hands and bind them on your foreheads. Teach them to your children, talking about them when you sit at home and when you walk along the road, when you lie down and when you get up. Write them on the doorframes of your houses and on your gates, so that your days and the days of your children may be many... See, I am setting before you today a blessing and a curse – the blessing if you obey the commands of the Lord your God that I am giving you today, the curse if you disobey the commands of the Lord your God..." (Deut. 11:1, 8, 9, 18-21, 26-28)

The mainstream Christian church has a perception problem with these words of the Torah. They consider it a 'strange thing'.

> **"I have written to him the great things of My Torah (law), but they were counted as a strange thing."** (Hos. 8:12)

The Torah is great, but Christianity considers it 'strange' and rejects it. Yeshua issued a declaration that we all need to heed. He said that many who call Him Lord and do great works in the Church, who even have deliverance and healing ministries, will be rejected by Him and not enter the kingdom.

> **"Not everyone who says to Me, 'Lord, Lord,' shall enter the kingdom of heaven, but he who does the will of My Father in heaven. Many will say to Me in that day, 'Lord, Lord, have we not prophesied in Your name, cast out demons in Your name, and done many wonders in Your name?' And then I will declare to them, 'I never knew you; depart from Me, you who practice lawlessness!'"** (Matt. 7:21-23)

This passage does not condemn the charismatic gifts. The word translated iniquity is the Greek word, *anomia*. *Noma* comes from *nomos*, which means law. The prefix *a-* means without. Therefore, Yeshua is rebuking those who operate in the gifts of the Spirit, but walk without the law or Torah. Oh, for the day that we would walk in a fullness of both the Torah and the Spirit. There is the danger of becoming unbalanced on either side.

Salvation by Grace

Of course none of us are without sin, and we depend on the grace of our merciful God for salvation.

> **"For there is not a righteous man upon earth who does good and sins not"** (Eccl. 7:20)

> **"But we are all like an unclean thing, and all our righteousness are like filthy rags."** (Is. 64:6)

The Torah was never given as a means of salvation. We are saved only by the blood of the Lamb, just as were the ancient Israelites also saved by the blood of the lamb and not by works in Egypt. But *after* our salvation, we need to be instructed in how to live as holy people unto God. The Torah is not discarded after our salvation. Many people are looking forward to the promised land but forget the pit-stop at Mount Sinai! Does our faith make void the Torah? No, it is established through our faith in Yeshua as our salvation.

> **"Do we then make void the law through faith? God forbid; yea we establish (keep) the law."** (Rom. 3:31)

I believe there is a big difference between 'salvation' and 'holiness'. Those who believe in and confess Yeshua may be on their way to heaven, but still defiled through their rebellion to the Torah.

> **"Blessed are the undefiled in the way, who walk in the law (Torah) of God."** (Ps. 119:1)

Yeshua is returning for an undefiled bride, a chaste virgin, one without spot or blemish.

> **"...That He might sanctify and cleanse her with the washing of water by the Word, that He might present her to Himself a glorious church, not having spot or wrinkle or any such thing, but that she should be holy and without blemish."** (Eph. 5:26, 27)

This means that the bride of Christ needs to mature in her walk with God to include obedience to Torah. Not everyone in the kingdom will be equal according to the words of Yeshua. (Matt. 5:19)

We depend upon the blood sacrifice of Yeshua, the Messiah, perfect in righteousness, to cleanse us from all sin. If you have never received forgiveness for your sins, and salvation from a holy God through Yeshua, I urge you to pray a prayer such as this from your heart:

> *"God of Israel, of Abraham, Isaac, and Jacob, please forgive me of all my sins, those revealed and also those hidden that only You know. Please also forgive my disobedience to Your Torah through the blood of your Son, Yeshua, the Messiah, and cleanse me from all unrighteousness. Fill me with Your Spirit that I may obey You and walk in Your ways. Thank You for the gift of eternal life. Amen."*

Note: If you prayed this prayer, and would like to contact the author, receive additional information, or subscribe to our newsletter, please visit our website: www.voiceforisrael.com or write to publisher. Several books, videos, and audiocassettes on Israel and the Hebraic Roots of the Christian Faith are available.

There is a huge difference, however, between obedience in order to be saved, and obedience because we are saved. We can stop and remember to thank and praise God at this time of Shavuot for all that He has done for us – for His bountiful provision, for choosing us and giving us His wonderful laws and commandments, showing us the ways of righteousness. Also, at this same time of Shavuot, we thank God for sending us His Holy Spirit, to lead and guide us into all truth and to anoint us to gather in this final harvest of souls into His kingdom.

CHAPTER SIX

RE-DISCOVERING TORAH

Shavuot can be an occasion to re-commit oneself to the study of and obedience to God's commandments. Wouldn't this seem like an appropriate time for the people of God to re-discover the Torah, the Word of God? After all, Yeshua the Messiah is the living Torah, the Word that became flesh and lived with us.

> **"In the beginning was the Word, and the Word was with God, and the Word was God. He was with God in the Beginning... The Word became flesh and made His dwelling among us."** (John 1:12, 14)

This is not the only period in history in which the Torah of God has been ignored, and pagan customs of the nations accommodated. Under the reign of King Hoshea, Israel was taken captive by Assyria and led into exile for her sins. Although the Lord warned the people through His prophets to change, they would not listen, just as most people are not listening today.

> **"'Turn from your evil ways. Observe My commands and decrees, in accordance with the entire Torah that I commanded**

> your fathers to obey and that I delivered
> to you through My servants the prophets.'
> But they would not listen and were as stiff-
> necked as their fathers, who did not trust
> in the Lord their God... They imitated the
> nations around them although the Lord
> had ordered them, 'Do not do as they
> do,' and they did the things the Lord had
> forbidden them to do." (2 Kin. 17:13-15)

I plead with you, through this writing, to seek the Lord about these matters with a sincere and open heart and mind, rather than being stiff-necked by walking in the ways of previous generations, which have ignored the law of God.

> "A man who remains stiff-necked after
> many rebukes will suddenly be destroyed
> – without remedy." (Prov. 29:1)

This is what happened to Israel. It stands as a lesson and a warning to all of us. We cannot make up our own religion, our own festivals, our own diets, our own Sabbath, and our own rules for righteous living apart from the Word of God without going seriously astray. Although it can be painful and sometimes difficult to follow God and live differently than 'the world', the alternative brings severe and perhaps irreversible consequences. The Lord warned us to count that cost before committing to follow Him – to be 'people of the way'. This may mean radical changes in our lives. An ancient, Hebrew king named Josiah was one such radical.

Hilkiah, the high priest under King Josiah, found the Book of the Law (Sefer HaTorah) in the temple of the Lord. He gave it to Shaphtan, the secretary, who read from it in the presence of the king. What was the king's reaction? He tore his robes in grief and repentance, knowing that the Lord's anger burned against them for ignoring His Word.

> **"Great is the Lord's anger that burns against us because our fathers have not obeyed the words of this book; they have not acted in accordance with all that is written there concerning us."** (2 Kin. 22:11-13)

Because of this great leader's responsive heart, and because he humbled himself before the Lord on his own and his people's behalf because of their disobedience to Torah, God showed them mercy. Where are the leaders of congregations and churches today who will hear the words of the Book of the Torah and humble themselves with responsive hearts and who will lead their congregations into obedience in this day?

King Josiah responded wholeheartedly – not just with words, but with radical action. Repentance, to this righteous leader, did not merely consist of a prayer and perhaps a few tears shed at a Sunday evening meeting. The king called together all the elders, gathered all his people, and read in their hearing the words of the 'Book of the Covenant'. The king, in the presence of his people, and the Lord, renewed his commitment to:

> **"Follow the Lord and keep His commands, regulations and decrees with all his heart and all his soul, thus confirming the words of the covenant written in this book."**
> (2 Kin. 23:13)

The people followed his lead.

> **"Then all the people pledged themselves to the covenant."** (2 Kin. 23:3)

One of his first acts was to remove all pagan symbols and articles and to burn them – everything that had caused his people to sin. We may be required to wait a long time, perhaps until the coming of the Lord, for our leaders to stand up against sin and paganism within Christianity in this way, but we can individually cleanse our lives and homes. This may require a thorough and prayerful search for elements of those things that are pagan and not biblical. Josiah also ordered the celebration of Passover. This, also, can be celebrated in our own homes and in groups, rather than participating in the pagan festival of Easter.

Josiah also got rid of mediums, spiritists, idols, and other detestable things. Far too many Bible believing, church-going people are dabbling in the occult – astrology, mind-control, meditation, yoga, psychics, and other 'New Age' infiltration into Christianity from Eastern mysticism. This is a major end time deception that will cause many people to fall under the influence of the coming anti-Christ.

I vividly remember struggling with the conviction to confront the management of a neighbourhood coffee shop about a sign in the window advertising psychic readings. Gathering up whatever faltering courage I could muster, Bible in hand, I set out to show them the Word of God and to warn them against allowing psychics to peddle their occultism in their place of business. When I spoke to the owner about this matter, she stood there speechless for a moment, before confessing that she, as well as all her staff were believers. It was my turn to stand in shocked silence. How is this compromise of our faith happening? By disregarding Torah, the Word of God. After all, if a little compromise with the paganism of the nations is acceptable, then why not jump right into Egypt?

If the Messiah has delivered us from spiritual 'Egypt', why do we choose to return? It was the blood of the Passover lamb on the doorposts of the people of Israel that saved them from the wrath of God, but they were required to actually apply the blood to their homes and then to remain sheltered under that blood covering. Had they merely confessed their faith in the blood of the lamb, but not applied it, it would have been of no benefit to save. Also, if they had applied the blood, but then sent their firstborn to walk the streets of Egypt on that night of judgment, they too would have been destroyed. So, too, we cannot merely confess our faith in the Messiah and think that is sufficient. This faith must make a difference in our lives. We cannot 'walk the streets of Egypt' and still expect to be saved.

Our children are also being very cleverly and deliberately indoctrinated to accept New Age doctrines and the Eastern religious teachings in the name of 'unity' and 'world peace'. Most Disney movies today contain much sorcery, magic, mysticism, New Age, Greek gods and occultism. Even some innocent children's cartoons promote ungodly attitudes such as, 'You can always trust your feelings' and project little bears visiting Hindu gurus and mystics and following the 'Tao'. Many churches, I am sad to report, celebrate some form of Halloween – holding costume parties for the children - thinking that as long as they don't dress up as little ghoulies and goblins, witches and warlocks, they are still A-1 before God. If one is participating in a demonic party, it is still of the kingdom of darkness, even if one doesn't dress the part.

In one church where we were teaching a Sunday evening series on the Jewish Roots of Christianity, alternate class down the hall was carving pumpkins for Halloween. Since some of the people in this church heard the truth and began asking questions and requiring change, the pastor confessed he wished we had never taught the course. Oh, for pastors who will stand for the truth! But God always has a remnant. May you be included in that faithful remnant! Many Jewish people today, most of whom have not actually read the Torah, writings, and prophets, also disregard God's Word against occultism and are in danger of falling into this end time deception. Israelis are so fixated against the pagan form of Christianity we see today, that they are almost completely ignoring the threat of New Age occultism that is sweeping the country.

A young student of mine, a typical Israeli teenager, continually came to his weekly English lesson with a representation of an 'alien' tied around his neck. Finally one week, I could remain silent no longer. With my less than fluent Hebrew and his less than fluent knowledge of scripture, I told him that this necklace of his was bad (rah). He asked why, since his brother in Australia had given it to him. I told him that it was against God (neged Elohim). Again, he asked why, since he had worn it to the Beit Knesset (synagogue) and no one commented on it. Almost laughing now, I told him that most at the Beit Knesset don't know about it either.

"But why is it against God?" he wanted to know.

"Oh, it must be something about Yeshu" (the derogatory name for Yeshua most Jewish people use), he said, making the sign of the cross with his fingers. How sad, I thought to myself, that the first thing a typical Israeli thinks of as being 'against God' is Jesus and Christianity.

This is why I believe returning to a biblically based faith in the God of Abraham, Isaac, and Jacob; the God of Israel, through Yeshua the Messiah is so crucial. What was lost must be restored – and quickly! I assured this Israeli boy that aliens do not have anything to do with Christianity. I told him, very simply, that there is a kingdom of light and of goodness, which belongs to God; and that there is a kingdom of darkness and evil with belongs to HaSatan (the adversary), and that there is an ongoing battle between the two kingdoms.

"Yes, but God is the winner!" he said, raising his fist in victory.

"True", I agreed, but aliens belong to the darkness, and we must show that we are on God's side, not on the side of darkness. Understanding these simple concepts, he immediately removed the necklace. I told him to share this knowledge with others he sees wearing symbols of darkness on their T-shirts and jewelry. This is our mission – to rescue people from darkness, those headed for destruction – and turn them back to God.

The Final Triumph of the Torah

In the end, we know that Yeshua will have the victory, and Torah will be taught from Zion to God-fearing people from many nations.

> **"In the last days, the mountain of the Lord's temple will be established as chief among the mountains; it will be raised above the hills, and all nations will stream to it. Many peoples will say, 'Come, let us go up to the mountain of the Lord, to the house of the God of Jacob. He will teach us His ways, so that we may walk in His paths.' The law (Torah) will go out from Zion, the Word of the Lord from Jerusalem."** (Is. 2:2, 3)

Israel Returning to the Kingdom

A foreshadow of this is taking place right now, as the Lord is raising up Messianic Jewish believers to go forth and teach people of many nations the ways of God. This process also took place in ancient times, as described in 2 Kings 17. After Israel's exile because of sin, Samaria was resettled with foreigners. (v.24) These people did not worship the Lord, nor know what the God of Israel requires from His people; therefore they were being killed off by lions. (v.26) Today, we see many Christians falling prey to Satan, who prowls about like a roaring lion, seeking whom he may devour. This, I believe, is because they simply do not know what the God of Israel requires, nor are they being taught this in most Christian churches. Alarmed by the carnage, the King of Assyria ordered that some of the former Israelite 'cohanim' (Jewish priests), move back into the kingdom and live amongst the 'goyim' (Gentiles), in order to teach them the ways of God. (vs. 27-28)

The Olive Tree

Paul describes an olive tree, some of whose natural (Jewish) branches have been temporarily broken off in order that a wild olive shoot (Gentile) could be grafted in.

> **"If some of the branches have been broken off, and you, though a wild olive shoot, have been grafted in among the others and now share in the nourishing sap from the olive root, do not boast over those branches."**
> (Rom. 11:17, 18)

But, as Paul says, God is able to graft them in again.

> **"And if they do not persist in unbelief, they will be grafted in, for God is able to graft them in again. After all, if you were cut out of an olive tree that is wild by nature, and contrary to nature were grafted into**

> **a cultivated olive tree, how much more readily will these, the natural branches, be grafted into their own olive tree!"** (Rom. 11:23, 24)

This is what God is doing today – grafting Jewish people, the natural branches, back into their own olive tree, in order to teach the wild olive shoot the Torah. Have the Jewish people, even with their hardness of heart towards the gospel and towards God Himself, fallen beyond the point of recovery?

> **"Did they stumble beyond recovery? Not at all! Rather, because of their transgression, salvation has come to the Gentiles to make Israel envious. But if their transgression means riches for the world, and their loss means riches for the Gentiles, how much greater riches will their fullness bring! For if their rejection is the reconciliation of the world, what will their acceptance be but life from the dead?"** (Rom. 11:11-15)

Yes, we are in for exciting times – resurrection times – as more and more Jewish people accept salvation through Yeshua and heed the priestly call to teach Torah to the nations.

Strychnine Disguised as Candy

Did the new settlers in Israel accept the teaching of the cohanim? Well, the situation was much as it is today: to a certain extent (their comfort zone), they accepted the teaching, but beyond this point, they held onto their cherished pagan customs. It's not that they did not worship the Lord, and I am not implying that Christianity in its present form is not worshipping the Lord, but it is a worship of God without giving up their pagan customs.

> **"They worshipped the Lord, but they also served their own gods in accordance with the customs of the nations from which they had been brought. To this day they persist in their former practices... You must always be careful to keep the decrees and ordinances, the laws and commands He wrote for you...They would not listen, however, but persisted in their former practices. Even while these people were worshipping the Lord, they were serving their idols. To this day their children and grandchildren continue to do as their fathers did."** (2 Kin. 17:33-41)

I think we can safely say that this situation continues to exist in most Christian congregations today. The idolatry and paganism may be dressed up as Christianity, but under this surface veneer, it is still not of the kingdom of light. A bottle of strychnine with a candy wrapper glued to the label is still poisonous.

Jesus and Mary Statues Take Priority

Some of these books were being distributed at a Christian bookstore in Canada at one point. We approached the owner to assemble a display of Messianic Jewish books and materials such as these in his store. What was his reply? The store was due to receive a shipment of Jesus and Mary statues, which would take up most of the spare room available. Since this was a business, as well as a ministry, he must adjust his inventory to meet customer demand. Didn't his Christian customers heed the second of the Ten Commandments prohibiting idol worship? I asked. In fact, the statues of these 'saints' are only replicas of the representations of Greek, Egyptian, and other heathen gods such as Venus and Isis. Lord, have mercy on us all!

Shavuot traditionally begins a child's Jewish education. Let this feast mark the beginning of your discipleship in the ways of the Lord God of Israel! May you become like King David, who could say,

> **"Oh, how I love Your Torah! It is my meditation all the day... I hate the double-minded, but I love Your Torah... I hate and abhor lying, but I love Your Torah"** (Ps. 119:97, 113, 163)

May you be blessed as you come to delight in the Torah and enjoy prosperity on all your works as you meditate upon the Torah! May you be like a well-watered tree, always fruitful for the Kingdom of God!

> **"Blessed is the man...But his delight is in the Torah of YHVH, and in His Torah he meditates day and night. He shall be like a tree planted by the rivers of water; that brings forth its fruit in its season, whose leaf also shall not wither; and whatever he does shall prosper."** (Ps. 1:13)

Take heed that you keep your soul undefiled by walking in the Torah of God.

> **"Blessed are the undefiled in the way, who walk in the Torah of YHVH."** (Ps. 119:1)

Refuse to walk with the crowd, which strays from God's commandments through pride.

"You rebuke the proud – the cursed, who stray from Your commandments."
(Ps. 119:21)

You will likely encounter much opposition, ridicule, and persecution for walking in the Torah of God, but such was the treatment that Yeshua endured. And so we do not lose heart, for better to obey God rather than man. Better to receive the rebuke of man, than the rebuke of God.

"The proud have me in great derision, yet I do not turn aside from Your Torah."
(Ps. 119:51)

Take a lesson from God's dealings with ancient Israel. They were not sent into captivity for crucifying Jesus, as many believe, but for their disobedience to His Torah. (Deut. 28:15,41,58,64) We must not just hear this message, but also obey.

"For not the hearers of the law are just in the sight of God, but the doers of the law will be justified." (Rom. 2:13)

The Gentile who keeps the law (Torah) shows that his or her heart has truly been supernaturally circumcised by the Messiah. (Rom. 2:14, 15; Col. 2:11) This is the one who is a true Yehudite.

We need not be fooled by the lies of those who preach an unbalanced grace message, for the Word says that

> **"God will render to each one according to
> his deeds."** (Rom. 2:6)

Yeshua commanded us also to keep His commandments
in order to enter into eternal life.

> **"If you want to enter into life, keep the
> commandments."** (Matt. 19:17)

In the final analysis, it will only be those who love God
and keep His commandments who will have the right to
enter the New Jerusalem and eat of the tree of life.

> **"Blessed are those who do His
> commandments, that they may have
> the right to the tree of life, and may
> enter through the gates into the city."**
> (Rev. 22:14)

If this is the final word of the final chapter of the entire
bible, then we would do well to heed its message. May God
bless you with a double portion of His Spirit, to empower
you to keep His great Torah! Shalom.

APPENDIX

The Ten Commandments

"I am the LORD your God, who brought you out of the land of Egypt, out of the house of bondage. You shall have no other gods before Me.

You shall not make for yourself a carved image of any likeness of anything that is in heaven above, or that is in the earth beneath, or that is in the water under the earth. You shall not bow down to them nor serve them. For I, the LORD your God am a jealous God, visiting the iniquity of the fathers upon the children to the third and fourth generations of those who hate Me, but showing mercy to thousands, to those who love Me and keep My commandments. You shall not take the name of the LORD your God in vain, for the LORD will not hold him guiltless who takes His name in vain.

Remember the Sabbath day, to keep it holy. Six days you shall labor and do all your work, but the seventh day is the Sabbath of the LORD your God. In it you shall do no work: you, nor your son, nor your daughter, nor your male servant, nor your female servant, nor your cattle, nor your stranger who is within your gates. For in six days the LORD made the heavens and the earth, the sea, and all that is in them, and rested the seventh day. Therefore the LORD blessed the Sabbath day and hallowed it.

Honor your father and your mother, that your days may be long upon the land which the LORD your God is giving you.

You shall not murder.

You shall not commit adultery.

You shall not steal.

You shall not bear false witness against your neighbor.

You shall not covet your neighbor's house; you shall not covet your neighbor's wife, nor his male servant, nor his female servant, nor his ox, nor his donkey, nor anything that is your neighbor's."

BIBLIOGRAPHY

Chumney, Eddie, *'Who is the Bride of Christ'*, Serenity Books, 1997

Koster, C.J., *'Come Out of Her My People'*, Institute for Scripture Research, 1986

Berkowitz, Ariel and D'vorah, *'Torah Rediscovered'*, First Fruits of Zion

NIV *'Life Application Bible'*, Tyndale House Publishers, Inc. Wheaton Illinois, and Zondervan Publishing House, 1984

Botkin, D., *'Gates of Eden'*, Nov-Dec 2000, PO Box 2257, East Peoria, IL 61611.0257 Vol. 6 No. 6

Katz, Art, Apostolic Foundations, *'The Challenge of Living an Authentic Christian Life'*

Stern, David H., *'Restoring the Jewishness of the Gospel'*, Jewish New Testament Publications

Prager, Dennis and Telushkin, Jospeh, *'The Nine Questions People Ask About Judaism'*

Chaimberlin, Rick Aharon Litt.D, *'The "Conversion" of Saul of Tarsus'*, Petach Tikvah (Door of Hope), Jan-March 2001, vol. 19, No. 1, p. 21. 165 Doncaster Road, Rochester, NY, 14623, USA

To contact the Author write:

Hannah Nesher, Voice for Israel
Suite #313- 11215 Jasper Ave.
Edmonton, Alberta
T5K 0L5 Canada

www.voiceforisrael.net

*Please include your testimony or help
received from this book when you write.*

Your prayer requests are welcome

Additional Teaching Materials by Hannah Nesher

DVDs

Shalom Morah I (Hebrew for Christians & Hebrew Names of God) 11 DVD set

Shalom Morah II (Hebrew for Christians & Wisdom in the Hebrew Alphabet) 10 DVD set

Exploring the Jewish Roots of the Christian Faith

Unity in the Messiah

Because He Lives

Messianic Jewish Wedding in Jerusalem

There is a God in Israel

Messianic Jewish Passover

Passover Lamb or Easter Ham?

Voice Out of Zion II (Where is Your Brother Jacob?)

Walking Through the Wilderness

Ruth: A Righteous Gentile

Messiah in Chanukah

BOOKS

Grafted in Again

Journey to Jerusalem

Come Out of Her My People

Messiah Revealed in Purim

Messiah Revealed in the Sabbath

Messiah Revealed in Passover

Messiah Revealed in the Fall Feasts

Messiah Revealed in Chanukah

Kashrut: The Biblical Dietary Laws

You Know My Heart (English booklet)

You Know My Heart (Hebrew booklet)